LIBRARIES AND TECHNICAL INFORMATION DIVISION
General Editor: G. CHANDLER

HOW TO FIND OUT ABOUT
SHAKESPEARE

DISCARD

HOW TO FIND OUT ABOUT

SHAKESPEARE

BY

JOHN BATE
M.A.(Hons.), Dip.Ed., F.L.A.

*Librarian, Napier College of Science and Technology,
Edinburgh*

1966
THE QUEEN'S AWARD
TO INDUSTRY 1966

PERGAMON PRESS

OXFORD · LONDON · EDINBURGH · NEW YORK
TORONTO · SYDNEY · PARIS · BRAUNSCHWEIG

Pergamon Press Ltd., Headington Hill Hall, Oxford
4 & 5 Fitzroy Square, London W.1
Pergamon Press (Scotland) Ltd., 2 & 3 Teviot Place, Edinburgh 1
Pergamon Press Inc., 44–01 21st Street, Long Island City, New York 11101
Pergamon of Canada Ltd., 207 Queen's Quay West, Toronto 1
Pergamon Press (Aust.) Pty. Ltd., 19a Boundary Street, Rushcutters Bay,
N.S.W. 2011, Australia
Pergamon Press S.A.R.L., 24 rue des Écoles, Paris 5ᵉ
Vieweg & Sohn GmbH, Burgplatz 1, Braunschweig

Printed in Great Britain by A. Wheaton & Co., Exeter

FOR M.M.B.

All dues be render'd to their owners
This time it is husband to the wife

Contents

List of Illustrations

Introduction

THIS short guide to the study of the plays and poetry of William Shakespeare is a librarian's contribution. The librarian's role is to act as a go-between, to bring the work of the expert to the attention of the inexpert; he tries to find the right book for the right reader at the right time, as has been said so often before. In this book I seek to help the beginner, the young student, or the young teacher, embarking on Shakespeare studies. I have a sufficiently long experience as a librarian not to overestimate the skill and learning of the student but have never ost my respect for his intellectual vigour and ardent insights. I hope, therefore, that my presentation of the field of Shakespeare studies may be found readily comprehensible, and that I have not over-clogged my text with references. The first book to be read in any campaign of study is like the first shot to be fired in a battle—it leads inevitably to many others. If I can communicate the enthusiasm of the writers of the books I name for the study of Shakespeare, I shall be content.

I have not attempted to follow in detail any of the several systems that have been worked out to classify books about Shakespeare, such as the British Museum scheme, the Library of Congress scheme, or that adopted by the British National Bibliography, although the order of my chapters follows broadly the same pattern as is discernible in these schemes. I have sought to give in each case sufficient information about a book or periodical article for it to be traced in a library catalogue, or in one of the indexes to periodicals, or for a bookseller to run it to earth in his reference catalogues of books in print.

A friend urged me recently to read Marshall McLuhan's *The Gutenberg Galaxy*, a work not at present as well known on the

European side of the Atlantic as it is likely one day to be. The chapter headings such as 'The print-made split between head and heart is the trauma which affects Europe from Machiavelli till the present' or 'The divorce of poetry and music was first reflected by the printed page' are arresting. Equally striking is the statement: "The printing press was at first mistaken for an engine of immortality by everybody except Shakespeare"—the Shakespeare, that is, who "couldn't be bothered to print his plays"—I asked myself for the first time whether perhaps Shakespeare's failure to have his plays printed was not just a strange oversight on his part, but a deliberate decision. In this case his lines

> How would he look, to see his work, so noble,
> Vilely bound up

would refer, not as Dr. Johnson supposed in his witty comment, to a Binder, but to the Printer, who by "binding" the words to the page would in some way falsify them. Did Shakespeare's understanding of life, or society and of man take him beyond the world of print; in which case, how is one to find out about Shakespeare by reading one's way through all the monstrous mountain of print that has accumulated about his life, his work, and the society in which he lived?

Marshall McLuhan's work on understanding media, with particular reference to the role of print in shaping man's ideas about himself, must obviously be given weight in any study of so great a master of the art of communication as Shakespeare. I think it will be clear from the works I cite that many modern scholars are insistent that Shakespeare can only be truly known when performed on the stage, and a stage, moreover, which resembles that on which his plays were first performed. There is no doubt that "the play's the thing". If you wish to find out about Shakespeare, the only way is through the performance of his plays on stage or screen, whether as a spectator or as an actor. The communication is in the unfolding of the drama. It is not possible, however, to take a copy of the First Folio and from this text to perform the plays. There is a very great deal more involved than that, and the plan of my book is to unfold to the reader just how much more there is. I have sought to guide the diligent inquirer into the heart of the most detailed and scholarly investigation, but to do this in such a way as to interest also the students who have only the time to acquaint themselves with the rudiments of the subject. There are, after all, getting on for 40,000 volumes in the Shakespeare Memorial Library in Birmingham, and I cannot mention in the small compass of this book more than about 400 of them. How can a selection of 1 in 100 be justified, except to say that those which are selected, when consulted, will themselves lead on to those which are not.

My plan, therefore, is to begin with the England in which Shakespeare lived, to develop a sense of his times, the ideas, and the political and social tensions of his England; to turn next to the events of his life and the doubts that have been cast on his very existence; then to look at the theatre in which he earned his living and won his fame. How has the text of his plays come down to us —what sources did he use? Then on to the literary criticism of his works, taking the general criticism first, then criticism of different types, followed by a selection of special themes and subjects as dealt with by Shakespeare. A short chapter deals with the sonnets and poems, and the two final chapters are aids to the use of libraries—one outlining a method of finding material on the individual plays and the other describing the main bibliographical tools for the study of Shakespeare. I have had in mind the needs of those trying to build up their own small personal libraries and the needs of teachers with school collections to nourish and foster as well as for all those students with essays to write, and long lists of recommended reading, who seek a guide to the contents of the library shelves in university or college.

I do not think it is for the librarian to make critical assessments of works of learning unless he himself is a specialist, apart from commenting on the actual physical appearance; if, therefore, I have been led into using at times unguarded evaluative epithets, I must ask the indulgence of scholars for my intrusion into their world. I have limited my quotations from the books mentioned to extracts which indicate as briefly as possible the author's intentions in writing the work concerned. To give my bibliography a narrative interest I have attempted to describe together works with similar viewpoints, and to confront these with books of an opposing tendency. This I have done in accord with what can be discovered of the burden of a work from a reading of the author's own declared aims in writing it.

Consistency has presented some problems; some authors prefer "Shakespeare" and some "Shakspere"; some "Shakespearean" and some "Shakespearian", but I have followed in every case the spelling adopted in the book quoted. I have sought to be up to date and correct with the academic rank of the authors whose works I cite, but have not thought it necessary to use this rank in every mention of an author by name. Sometimes a recently acquired title would conceal an identity, so I have used the more familar name. I have printed in italics all titles of books, including the titles of Shakespeare's plays; in single inverted commas the titles of articles and papers, and in double inverted commas all quotes from any of the works mentioned.

I have only dated books where it seems necessary to do so, as when some such word or phrase as "present day" occurs in a title, or when there has been more than one edition with some considerable difference in the text of the later.

Throughout his works Shakespeare is preoccupied with the effects of time upon man and his society, and he expresses both his acceptance of time's ravages and his determination to defeat them:

> Thy registers and thee I both defy,
> Not wond'ring at the present, nor the past,
> For thy records, and what we see doth lie,
> Made more or less by thy continual haste:
>> This I do vow and this shall ever be,
>> I will be true despite thy scythe and thee.

He knew that in the end

>> the great globe itself,
> Yea, all which it inherit, shall dissolve,
> And like this insubstantial pageant faded,
> Leave not a rack behind:

and this knowledge should give the patient bibliographer a sense of proportion.

Like all authors I have been helped by many people; I should like to mention particularly the staff of the National Library of Scotland for their unfailing patience and courtesy and the Librarian of the Shakespeare Memorial Library, Birmingham; also Dr. S. W. Wells of The Shakespeare Institute, and to Mr. Fred Turner of the University of California, Santa Barbara, for useful advice. I am also greatly indebted to my daughter, Sophie, for all kinds of practical assistance, and to my wife for shielding me from family responsibilities while in the toils of composition; and, last but not least, to Miss Margaret Anderson, for re-typing my first, disorderly draft, and to my children Lucy and Robin, for their help (well rewarded) with the Index.

CHAPTER I

Shakespeare's England

THE pastoral and mercantile England of the time of Shakespeare, with its total population unlikely to have exceeded 3 million, was a very different country from the slowly choking bustle of today's 55 million, although there is little about ourselves of value that we cannot learn from a study of Shakespeare's works.

There is available a numerous library of books about Elizabethan England, the political and social life of that unforgettable time. Here I have selected a few that vividly and with immediacy explain the results of detailed research.

Nowhere can a more precise knowledge of that "order of society" be gained than in the pages of A. L. Rowse's *The England of Elizabeth: the structure of society*. Here are chapters on the land, its ownership, tenancy, use, and state; on London and the towns; on government and administration; on the Church and religion—a most carefully organized reconstruction made possible by the study of contemporary documents and records. There is at the beginning of the book a most interesting chapter on 'The Elizabethan discovery of England', about the work of the topographers, in which Rowse writes that "the increasing self-consciousness of the nation may be regarded as the fruit of the twin impulses of Renaissance and Reformation".

The two volumes that were prepared by C. T. Onions for the tercentenary celebration of Shakespeare's death, which were published in 1916, brought together work by many outstanding scholars of that day under the title *Shakespeare's England*. The purpose of the book is "to describe the habits of the English people during Shakespeare's lifetime". It is in the accounts of the lesser activities that the book excels, and the chapter by R. B. McKerrow on 'Booksellers, printers and the stationers' trade' and that by Sir E. Maunde Thompson on 'Handwriting' are very well known. But there are chapters on folk lore, superstition, plants, animals, heraldry, London life, and most scholarly, on 'Shakespeare's English' by the grammarian, Henry Bradley. There are many excellent full-plate illustrations.

A more popular book, presented also by an eminent scholar, namely Louis B. Wright, Director of the Folger Shakespeare Library, is called *Shakespeare's England* as well. It is a colourful production plentifully illustrated with paintings, drawings, and engravings of the period: "The purpose of the book is not to challenge the debatable points of Shakespeare's biography or to probe his literary reputation. It is rather, to present the playwright as a man of his day against the colourful tapestry of his England, the kingdom under Elizabeth I and James I"—a timely reminder this, that Shakespeare lived 13 years as a Jacobean. The illustrations in this book include a painting purporting to be of Jonson and Shakespeare playing chess, Jonson bare-headed and square, Shakespeare wearing a broad-brimmed hat, his handsome, elfin features alert and intelligent. Doubts have been cast on the authenticity of the painting, but the author of this book thinks that it may well have been taken from the life. There is also a photograph of a model made for the film of Olivier's *Henry V*, showing the site of the Globe Theatre in the London of the sixteenth century, rising bluntly from the midst of an orchard.

The Folger booklets on Tudor and Stuart civilization have been appearing for some years, and a collection of some of them has been published as *Life and Letters in Tudor and Stuart England: first Folger series*, edited by Louis B. Wright and Virginia A. La Mar. These essays cover such topics as England's Elizabeth, its government, life of Shakespeare, authorship problems; as well as theatre, music, Bible and Church, schools and universities, and dress, sport, and recreations. The authors are American and English scholars of note.

No one is a more vivid re-creator of the life of a vanished epoch than C. V. Wedgwood. Her paper in the collection *Shakespeare's World*, edited by James Sutherland and Joel Hurstfield from the scripts of nine lectures given at University College, London, to commemorate the fourth centenary of Shakespeare's birth, is a valuable contribution, though brief. The other papers deal with some of the major aspects of his work and with his critical reputation; they are addressed to an audience not drawn exclusively from students of the period.

To know the Elizabethans, let them speak for themselves. Allardyce Nicoll collected 421 extracts from the writings of contemporaries of Shakespeare and published them in a book entitled *The Elizabethans*, the text being illustrated on nearly every page with reproductions from the period. A great range of subjects is covered, from government and the Church to home and school life. There are fascinating sections on the army and navy, on travel and recreations, roads and inns, rogues and vagabonds, witches and fairies. The extracts are printed in a numbered sequence with a list at the end of the book identifying each one with notes on the authorship.

Many documents have been reproduced in an interesting publication in the Jackdaw series of historical facsimiles, entitled *Young Shakespeare: a collection of contemporary documents*. The compiler is John Langdon-Davies.

Ivor Brown has written a book of 48 large pages entitled *Shakespeare and His World*, containing illustrations drawn from contemporary sources which, together with the text, give a plain account of life in Shakespeare's England. Ivor Brown gives a salutary reminder of the precarious profession of the playwright in those days:

> His fame has spread so widely and has risen so high that we may think of him as a very important person in his own lifetime. That he was not. The actors were under the protection of the Court and of some noblemen who enjoyed the entertainment which they provided. Without that protection they could not have acted at all and Shakespeare might have been driven into some other profession. For play-acting was despised and even hated by many prominent citizens in the merchant class of the City of London who regarded the theatre as a sinful place and the players as corrupters of the people.

Not so attractively presented as these books, but providing all the same a most absorbing series of extracts from the writings of Elizabethans of all types and degrees is J. Dover Wilson's *Life in Shakespeare's England.* A shorter account of the period is to be found in chapters VI and VII of G. M. Trevelyan's pioneering work *English Social History.*

There is no more devoted student of Shakespeare today than F. E. Halliday. His works are mentioned frequently in this guide, and in this chapter his *Shakespeare in His Age* must find an important place. He writes:

> I have tried to place myself in the position of Shakespeare, and describe the things that he saw, the plays and music that he heard, the books that he read, the men whom he met and the ideas that he encountered; and to weave into a single narrative the main political events of the period, the progress of the arts—architecture, painting and music, as well as poetry and the drama—the development of the theatre, and the fortunes of the dramatic companies.

The book is illustrated from contemporary sources. Vivid details maintain the interest. For instance, Halliday tells us that in 1564, the year of Shakespeare's birth, Galileo and Christopher Marlowe were also born and that Michelangelo and Calvin died; that Queen Elizabeth became owner of the first coach to be built in Britain and that John Hawkins brought back tobacco from the Spanish Main. He describes Marlowe demolishing the "clowns' and grocers' drama" and setting up the "drama of poets" despite the "normally restless, unruly and caterwauling audience". He reminds us that when Shakespeare was dying, William Harvey was delivering his lectures on the circulation of the blood and Inigo Jones preparing his drawings for the Queen's house at Greenwich, while in Madrid Cervantes was receiving the sacrament of extreme unction, and at Whitehall John Donne, the poet Shakespeare had so much envied, was preaching his first Court sermon. Here, indeed, is a memorable tapestry, most memorably woven.

C. J. Sisson, in his book *Lost Plays of Shakespeare's Age*, relates the drama of those times to contemporary events. F. P. Wilson, in his *The Plague in Shakespeare's London*, deals with the scourge that dogged the whole of Shakespeare's career as a dramatist and caused more deaths and suffering than any war of the period. *The English People on the Eve of Colonisation, 1603–1630*, by W. Notestein, a social historian, is a guide to the Jacobean years of Shakespeare's career.

In 1964, the fourth centenary year of Shakespeare's birth, *Shakespeare Survey 17*, edited by Allardyce Nicoll, was published; a magnificently comprehensive volume, subtitled *Shakespeare in His Own Age*. The editor wrote that "in the planning of this book an effort has been made to select themes which have been neglected, or which have received comparatively little attention, or which, although surveyed in the past, appeared to demand reappraisal". The book is arranged in three sections; the first deals with the physical environment—the life of London and the Court; provincial life; life at sea; the attitude to foreigners; education and apprenticeship; the law and London's prisons. The second section outlines the prevailing ideas in the thought of the period—political, scientific, medical—and the importance of symbols. The third section concerns art and entertainment—the language of Elizabethan England, the theatres and music, and the printing of books. The volume is illustrated with a fine series of reproductions of contemporary drawings and illustrations from books. One of the most interesting insights in this volume is its account of what can only be called the availability of adult education in London; a contemporary, Sir George Buck, in his *Third University of England*, is quoted as writing:

> I saw that not only those arts which are called liberal, but also all or the most part of all other arts and sciences proper and fit for ingenuous and liberal persons were and are in this city professed, taught, and studied: which is (adding but *cum privilegio*) as much as can be said for the name and authority of any university, and which can be rightly said of very few other universities in Christendom.

In the chapter on 'Dissent and satire' Barnard Harris writes of the confusion and dismay of the Roman Catholics and the Puritans, and sees the Stratford of Shakespeare's formative years as a town as divided as the rest of the country, quoting as evidence the careers of local notables. He writes: "The old religion was in retreat in Stratford, and Puritan dominance in local affairs was becoming evident, most markedly shown by the ban upon players visiting the town in 1602." Shakespeare refers little to the religious dissent of the times: "His stage church is medieval, not that of the counter-reformation or the reformed religion; and Malvolio is no Puritan." Again, in the chapter on 'Elizabethans and foreigners', G. K. Hunter reminds us that few Elizabethans had met a Jew or a Turk or a Moor; yet, as W. Besant wrote in his *London in the Time of the Tudors*, "Shakespeare could stir the blood of his audience by the spectacle of a Jewish usurer, three hundred years after there had been Jews in the land". And the explanation which follows is from Dr. H. Michelson's book *The Jew in Early English Literature*: "The New Testament and nothing but the New Testament is to be blamed for the peculiar psychology of the Jew in literature . . . down to and inclusive of Shylock this psychology was never based on observation, but simply taken over from the New Testament."

G. B. Harrison has collected various writings of Shakespeare's time into four entertaining volumes which he entitled *An Elizabethan Journal, 1591–94*; *A Second Elizabethan Journal, 1595–98*; *A Last Elizabethan Journal, 1599–1603*; and *A Jacobean Journal, 1603–1606*. A. H. Dodd's book *Life in Elizabethan England* and Muriel Byrne's *Elizabethan Life in Town and Country* are both informative and well illustrated. Joel Hurstfield, in *The Elizabethan Nation*, provides an admirably compressed account of Elizabeth's reign in four chapters. There are, of course, numerous works of historical scholarship. Two of these should be mentioned because they deal with the all-important maritime affairs of the nation. *The Age of Drake* by J. A. Williamson, which tells of the beginning of British expansion overseas, and *The Defeat of the Armada* by G. Mattingly. The Quennell's *Everyday Things in England*, in the appropriate volume, tells of the daily life of people of all classes.

Some scholars have found out a great deal about the town of Shakespeare's birth, notably E. I. Fripp, whose *Shakespeare's Stratford* and *Shakespeare's Haunts Near Stratford* are the fruit of painstaking investigations. Much learning has been pleasantly quarried in M. Eccle's *Shakespeare in Warwickshire*. Sir Sidney

Lee's *Stratford-on-Avon from Earliest Times to the Death of Shakespeare* provides a useful introduction to these works.

A popular book available in an illustrated paperback edition is John Russell's *Shakespeare Country*, a guide to the Stratford area of today; while an older book to be found still in many libraries is W. H. Hutton's *Highways and Byways in Shakespeare's Country*.

It was in London that Shakespeare made his name and fortune. John Stow's *Survey of London*, first published in 1598 when the Burbages were erecting a new Globe Theatre out of the ruins of the old, is the ideal book to read for an understanding of the city as Shakespeare knew it.

Next we must consider what Teilhard de Chardin would perhaps have called the Elizabethan no-osphere, the world of the mind in those days, discussed in E. M. W. Tillyard's *The Elizabethan World Picture* and Basil Willey's *The Seventeenth Century Background: studies in the thought of the age in relation to poetry and religion*. Tillyard says of his book:

> My object then is to extract and expound the most ordinary beliefs about the constitution of the world as pictured in the Elizabethan age and through this exposition to help the ordinary reader to understand and to enjoy the great writers of the age. In attempting this I have incidentally brought together a number of pieces of elementary lore which I have not found assembled elsewhere.

Basil Willey quotes T. S. Eliot's remark: "In attempting to win a full understanding of the poetry of a period you are led to the consideration of subjects which at first sight appear to have little bearing upon poetry." Although his book does not mention Shakespeare in the index, there is much in it, especially in the early chapters on Bacon and the rejection of scholasticism, that is of great interest to the student of Shakespeare's works.

A very interesting study of the intellectual climate of Shakespeare's time is *The Shakespearean Moment and its Place in the Poetry of the 17th Century* by Patrick Cruttwell. He writes: "The 1590's are intensely confused, precisely because the handing over was then taking place (between the pre and the post 1590 generations and mentalities); new and old were deeply entangled . . . but there *was* an old and there was a *new* and the task of criticism is to analyse and distinguish." This book pays particular attention to the Sonnets and the evidence they contain of Shakespeare's awareness of this watershed in thought, and to the influence of the young poet John Donne on the style and methods of the established playwright. Cruttwell writes: "In the last years of the 16th century, a new mentality was emerging, critical, dramatic, satirical, complex and uncertain; with it and part of it, came a new style in poetry to give it expression." Needless to say, Marshall McLuhan draws attention to this book, and reminds his readers that in our time we, too, are suffering confusion because our "older forms of perception and judgement are interpenetrated by the new electric age".

The American scholar T. W. Baldwin has published in two magnificent quarto volumes of 700 pages apiece a work entitled *William Shakespeare's Small Latine and Lesse Greeke* in which he sets out with wonderful spaciousness an account of Elizabethan education from Eton to the grammar schools, with a survey of the Latin grammar Shakespeare would have used and the Latin authors he would have studied at school. A little book by W. J. Rolfe called *Shakespeare the Boy* should also be mentioned.

CHAPTER 2

The Life of Shakespeare

SHAKESPEARE lived his life in the interval between two of the greatest social convulsions of English history, namely the Protestant Reformation of the early sixteenth century, and the Civil War of the mid seventeenth. The order and reason of the great Catholic middle ages was crumbling into ruins and the new and perhaps greater order and reason of the age of the enlightenment was yet to be born. It was an age, as G. M. Trevelyan says, when

> commerce was the motive of exploration as well as of warfare, and all three combined in some of the greatest deeds of that generation. Romance and money-making, desperate daring and dividends, were closely associated in the minds and hearts of men. There was no line drawn between the bread-and-butter facts of life, and the life of poetry and imagination.

Of all the books on the subject of Shakespeare's life, the one that seems to me to put most vividly the sense of the times, is F. E. Halliday's *Shakespeare: a pictorial biography*. The illustrations in this delightful book set the scene; the tree-lined Avon, serene and smooth; the worn stone of the square-built church with its elegant spire and its broad east window and long nave; the lush parklands and squat comfort of the homes of the country gentry; the lavish ornamentation of the stiff, formal clothes of the wealthy, both men and women; the heavy timbering of the grammar school room; the thatched Hathaway farmhouse at Shottery . . . it is all to be seen as well as read. There are 128 fastidiously chosen illustrations in this book, with an appendix of notes on each one. The text is straightforwardly written.

Nicholas Rowe, the first biographer of Shakespeare, is not mentioned by Mr. Halliday. This omission would appear to be deliberate because of all the wrong ideas about the poet for which he is accounted responsible. Another assiduous student of the life, Mr. Louis Marder, editor of the lively periodical *Shakespeare Newsletter*, seems to think that modern scholarship has added very little to the facts enumerated by Nicholas Rowe. In a fascinating article in a recent issue of his *Newsletter* he has suggested that up until now the searching of the public records by Shakespeare scholars has been unmethodical and many possible sources of information about Shakespeare have not been thoroughly examined. The sheer labour of reading through the mountain of manuscript, all in Elizabethan secretary hand, not easily mastered, has deterred the biographers. A good account of the present knowledge derived from the public records has been given by N. E. Evans of the Public Record Office in his *Shakespeare in the Public Records*. Mr. Marder reminds us of John Keats's comment. "Shakespeare led a life of allegory: his works are the commentary on it"—a remark whose profundity will leave ripples in the mind. Marder quotes the critic Ernest Brenecke on the biographies of Shakespeare, which he classifies as "factual; encyclopaedic-factual; factual-stylistical, commercial, dogmatical, inferential, and lexicographical; inferential-lunatical, autobiographical, fantastical, and fictional". Thus the inquiring student is warned.

Chief among the popular biographies is *William Shakespeare*, by the indefatigable Shakespearean, Ivor Brown. A shorter book by the same author, with copious illustrations, some in colour covering double pages, all helpfully evocative, is also entitled *William Shakespeare*, but intended for younger readers.

The fascination of Shakespeare's life is that none of his contemporaries told it, that hints of great crises in his personal affairs can be obtained from the plays and poems, and that there are a number of genuine puzzles, such as how did Shakespeare earn enough money in a decade and a half of playwriting to buy the best house in Stratford. The painstaking research of Sir E. K. Chambers makes his book *William Shakespeare: a study of facts and problems* the foundation of most modern biographical studies. The major part of this two-volume work is taken up with a consideration of the text of the plays. Volume 2 has transcripts of the documents which record major events in Shakespeare's life—his christening, his marriage, his will, his burial, and others. Charles Williams has produced an abridged version of this work, making its learning available to the less scholarly, under the title *A Short Life of Shakespeare with Sources*. E. K. Chambers himself published an invaluable little treatise at the end of his life, entitled *Sources for a Biography of Shakespeare*.

Edgar I. Fripp's *Shakespeare: man and artist* appeared in 1938, 7 years after the author's death, having been assembled from manuscript by Mr. F. C. Wellstood. The book is dense with authentic information. Fripp writes of his "passionate desire that Shakespeare be known and reverenced as a 'man' as well as 'artist'". His book studies and interprets Shakespeare in his environment, geographical, social, religious, dramatic, literary. A lifetime of devotion to the man Shakespeare, as well as to the poet and his works, enabled Fripp to build up a portrait that is compellingly clear.

In recent years, Professor Peter Alexander of Glasgow University has won worldwide renown for his edition of the complete works, published in 1951. As the fruit of his long studies on the text, he has produced a small book, entitled simply *Shakespeare*, which tells in its first 100 pages the story of Shakespeare's life under two main headings—firstly 'Stratford-on-Avon' and, secondly, 'London'. He enlivens his account by outlining scholarly opinion about such disputed matters as, for instance, that Shakespeare began his career by patching up other men's plays. Was the "upstart crow" that Greene referred to, an actor, and not a writer? Professor Alexander recommends as the best introduction to a study of Shakespeare's life and times, J. S. Smart's *Shakespeare: truth and tradition*, published in 1934. Another book widely recommended in the academic world is J. Dover Wilson's *The Essential Shakespeare: a biographical adventure*, of which the author writes: "Here in a nutshell is the kind of man I believe Shakespeare to have been." It is a nutshell of some 145 pages, of exquisite workmanship. But Wilson is himself a man of his time. He writes that "modern science, while reducing man to zero, has banished fear from his universe", comparing this state with that fearfulness of Shakespeare and his contemporaries that the heavenly bodies might "start madly from their spheres". It is a fear that in the 1960's man knows again only too well. When Laurence Olivier spoke those lines of Othello:

> But I do love thee! and when I love thee not,
> Chaos is come again—

what a chill horror clutched at the spines of the millions who heard them. Chaos is a spectre that haunts our age, as it haunted Shakespeare's, and his brave clarity of vision, and happy heart cheer us now, as they must have cheered those who knew and loved him during his life.

Himself no mean poet, the famous historian of the Elizabethan period, A. L. Rowse, has written a long and absorbing book, *William Shakespeare: a biography*, which is to be read with the greatest respect. The author makes but a modest claim, writing: "My hope was, as a historian, to be able to illuminate at least the history plays, the inspiration and treatment of England's past, by the most historically minded of dramatists—having spent a lifetime studying the period and the social life of Shakespeare's time." Another long and careful study is that of Peter Quennell, entitled *Shakespeare: the poet and his background*, which is "intended for the general student of literature and life, not for the stern Shakespearean student". It is a most learned and reliable narrative, pleasantly discursive, as in the chapter '*Romeo and Juliet*'. The themes of the play, the portrayal of minor characters like the Nurse, the performance in the Elizabethan theatre and the problems of a modern production, the references in other plays to the theme of sexual jealousy, are all discussed.

Hesketh Pearson was an inveterate biographer who produced entertaining lives of literary personalities, so it is not surprising that his *A Life of Shakespeare* is a heart-warming book though published in the depths of the Second World War. He prefaces the book with some telling quotations, as this from Samuel Johnson: "The stream of time, which is continually washing the dissoluble fabricks of other poets, passes without injury by the adamant of Shakespeare"; and this from H. G. Wells—"What did Shakespeare do? . . . He added no idea, he altered no idea, in the growing understanding of mankind." The book is very learned on such matters as the influence of Montaigne on the ideas in *Hamlet* and the events of the Gunpowder Plot, but it is all presented pleasingly and with no little wit.

Marchette Chute, in her frequently praised *Shakespeare of London*, attempts "to show William Shakespeare as his contemporaries saw him. He was once life size, and this is an attempt at a life size portrait." Her bibliography, which was compiled in 1951, lists 9 pages of recommended works. She has used for her book no evidence that is dated later than 1635, so her attempt at portraying Shakespeare as his contemporaries saw him has been made with the utmost rigour. Yet the narrative style of the book flows easily and naturally, as if Marchette Chute had grown up with Shakespeare and known him, and all the ins and outs of his life as well as if he were her favourite brother.

A long and detailed life, frequently recommended, is that written by Professor Joseph Quincy Adams of Cornell University, entitled *A Life of William Shakespeare*. The author was Director of the Folger Shakespeare Library for 15 years, but his *Life* was written before he began his work there.

Available in most libraries is the *Dictionary of National Biography* in which the 80 columns devoted to the life of Shakespeare were written by Sir Sidney Lee. His *Life of William Shakespeare*, published in 1898, was for many years considered to be the standard work on the subject, but its scholarship is nowadays, in the words of F. E. Halliday, "out of date".

Of the earlier twentieth-century lives, one still holds the reader by the sheer power of its prose: Sir Walter Raleigh's *Shakespeare* in the English Men of Letters series (1907).

Professor Gerald Eades Bentley, of Princeton, is the author of *Shakespeare: a biographical handbook*, a summary of all the available evidence. His chief concern was "to present the life of William Shakespeare and his methods of work with the strictest fidelity to the surviving documents, with the least personal bias and with a minimum of cultural bias of our time". Just how admirable the work of compression has been done can be assessed by comparing this handbook with the two magnificent large volumes published in 1940 by Professor B. Roland Lewis of the University of Utah, entitled *The Shakespeare Documents: facsimiles, transliterations, translations and commentary*.

Reading lives of Shakespeare gives one a desire to study *The Shakespeare Allusion Book*, a collection of allusions to Shakespeare from 1591 to 1700 in 2 volumes. This was originally compiled by C. M. Ingleby, Miss L. Toulmin Smith, and Dr. F. J. Furnivall (who founded the New Shakespeare Society and was responsible for the research which inspired Dowden's well-known *Shakspere: his mind and his art*). The work was re-edited, revised, and re-arranged with an introduction by John Munro and was again re-issued in 1932 with a preface by Sir Edmund Chambers.

Several interesting studies have been written of episodes in Shakespeare's life, one of the most well-known being that of Leslie Hotson, entitled *Shakespeare versus Shallow*, which is about the playwright's life in Southwark and his quarrel with the bullying J.P., William Gardiner, who caused the stage of the Swan Theatre to be torn down. Leslie Hotson also wrote *I, William Shakespeare*, re-creating a story of Shakespeare's friendships from the names of the persons mentioned in Shakespeare's will.

Arthur Acheson's *Shakespeare's Lost Years in London* is a study of the early years of his life in the capital city, stimulated by a reading of the eighteenth-century *Essay on the Dramatic Character of Sir John Falstaff* by Maurice Morgann who considered Shakespeare's characters rather as "Historic than as Dramatic beings". Another aspect of Shakespeare's life is treated in Ernest Law's *Shakespeare as Groom of the Chamber*, in which he gives an account of Shakespeare in the days of the conference of the English and Spanish Commissioners at Old Somerset House in 1604, when he was in-waiting.

Next, a mention of some of the novels that have been inspired by Shakespeare's life. *Sergeant Shakespeare*, written by the first Viscount Norwich, better known as Duff Cooper, in which the imaginary life of Shakespeare among the English troops in the Low Countries is entertainingly told. The many quotations from the plays demonstrate Shakespeare's accurate military knowledge and support the author's suppositions. Oscar Wilde wrote, perhaps for his own private propagandist purposes, *Portrait of Mr. W. H.*, but it is none the less entertaining for that. The most realistic of the novels is that by John Brophy, *Gentleman of Stratford*. Carola Oman, writer of monumental historical biographies, has used her powers subtly to portray *Best of His Family*, and Gerald Bullett, in his novel *Alderman's Son*, sets Shakespeare in his class and station, so important in the world of Elizabeth. Caryl Brahms and S. J. Simon provide a wisecracking commentary on a famous controversy in *No Bed for Bacon*. Other novels include *How Dark My Lady* by Ursula Bloom, *Whitely Wanton* by M. W. Disher, *One Grown with a Sun* by R. Holland, *Royal Players* by R. Payne, and *Remember Me* by F. S. Stuart.

But was Shakespeare himself a fiction? Or, at least, if he existed, could he have been the author of the sublime works attributed to him?

The evidence which scholars like Sir Edmund Chambers have gathered about the life of Shakespeare is strong despite the lack of any contemporary *Life*, or autobiographical fragments. Nevertheless, a doubt has existed and been fed by able minds that the works of William Shakespeare were written by someone else. Sir Arthur Bryant, the distinguished historian, says that it is almost a national pastime to suggest that our greatest poet was not the person we suppose him to have been. Mr. Ivor Brown insists that the man who wrote the greatest poetry in the English language must be known, especially as he lived in times otherwise so well documented. Thus a kind of detective puzzle has been created, which many think imaginary, but which none the less exercises a compelling fascination.

It has been estimated that something like 5000 works have been published on the Shakespeare authorship question, many of them

repetitious. None the less, Mr. R. C. Churchill publishes a formidable selected bibliography listing over 400 titles at the end of his
Shakespeare and His Betters which he describes as "a history and a
criticism of the attempts which have been made to prove that
Shakespeare's works were written by others". He considers first
the origins of the controversy, and then each of the various
theories in turn; that Shakespeare's works were written by a group
of authors; by Bacon; by Sir Walter Raleigh; by Edward de Vere,
17th Earl of Oxford; by William Stanley, 6th Earl of Derby; or by
any one of a number of notable individuals—Essex, Cecil, Burton,
Southampton, Shirley, Rutland, Barnard, Devonshire, Stirling,
Florio, Marlowe, or Elizabeth herself. He then makes out the case
against these theories in seven well-argued chapters.

The Baconian theory is supported by the well-known cipher
argument. Ignatius Donnelly's book *Great Cryptogram* covers
over 1000 pages, and Orville Owen's *Francis Bacon's Cipher Story*
needs 5 volumes to be told. As Mr. Churchill says, the Bacon
arguments can be divided into those that can only be understood
by the initiated and those that can be understood by ordinary
people. Perhaps the most readable of the works which are used by
the Baconians is Mark Twain's *Is Shakespeare Dead?*, which drew
attention to Shakespeare's will. This mentioned "not a play, not a
poem, not an unfinished literary work, not a scrap of manuscript
of any kind". The Baconians make much of the fact that the plays
show a remarkable technical knowledge of law, and this theme is
pursued in such works as *The Shakespeare Mystery* by Judge
Webb and *Shakespeare's Law* by Sir George Greenwood. An
amusing side-light is provided by the story of Delia Bacon, an
American woman of good family, who visited England when she
was 42 and persuaded the Vicar of Stratford to allow her to spend
a night in the church where Shakespeare's bones are buried. The
result of this proximity during the night were hallucinations in
which she received the notion that the plays were written by Bacon
and others. The story is told in Nathaniel Hawthorne's essay in
Our Old Home. One of the claims is that Bacon edited the First
Folio of 1623 (he lived until 1626) and caused the printer to insert

his ciphers. How this idea survives the work of the bibliographers who have identified every man on the composing staff of William Jaggard is a great mystery. As William F. Friedman and Elizebeth Friedman write in their book *The Shakespeare Ciphers Examined: an analysis of cryptographic systems used as evidence that some author other than William Shakespeare wrote the plays commonly attributed to him*: "Most scholars ignore or slight the theories of anti-Stratfordians. They are entitled to a courteous and—wherever possible—scientific examination of their arguments. It is in the case of cryptographic systems that this can most easily be done." And this they proceed to do in a handsome, closely reasoned book of over 300 pages.

Sir Walter Raleigh was executed in 1618. He spent many years in the Tower of London after his arrest on the orders of King James in July 1603; during this time he wrote his lengthy *History of the World*, so it is difficult to see how he could have supplied the voracious London theatre of those years with the many plays attributed to Shakespeare.

The theory that the author of the plays was William Stanley, 6th Earl of Derby, is most powerfully argued by Professor Lefranc, of the Collège de France in Paris, an authority on Rabelais. He is the only one of the hundreds of writers in this field who can claim the status of a professional literary scholar, for the authorship controversy seems to attract only those whose interest in Shakespeare is other than literary. None the less, the whole case is built up from two references found in the Calendar of State Papers. A recent work putting the case for Derby is Dr. A. W. Titherly's *Shakespeare's Identity: William Stanley, Sixth Earl of Derby*. As he lived until 1642, Derby kept his secret remarkably well.

The theory that the author of the plays was really Edward de Vere, the 17th Earl of Oxford, was proclaimed by J. Thomas Looney in his book "*Shakespeare*" *Identified in Edward de Vere*, a theory so startling that the publisher is reputed to have advised the author not to publish under his real name. Nevertheless, a Shakespeare fellowship was founded, as a result of the book's circulation, devoted to the study of the authorship question. Many works have proceeded from the members of this fellowship, perhaps the most notable being that by Louis P. Benezet, *Shakspere, Shakespeare and De Vere*, but the fact remains that the Earl died in 1604.

Mr. Churchill's *Shakespeare and His Betters* is a very fair presentation of the arguments of the supporters of the various contenders, although his conclusion makes it plain that he himself is not to be persuaded. He produces a fundamental argument, namely that the first suspicion that Shakespeare might be a mask for an aristocratic author arose in 1601, at the time of the ill-fated Earl of Essex's rebellion, when Shakespeare's company was prevailed upon to put on the play *Richard II*, with its highly suggestive deposition scene. The Privy Council knew that the play had been commissioned by the conspirators, and the remorseless investigator Topcliffe conducted an inquiry to discover whether the author of the play was implicated in the plot. Had Shakespeare not been proved to their satisfaction to be the real author, he would surely have been arrested until he revealed the name of the aristocrat he was concealing.

Frank W. Wadsworth's *The Poacher from Stratford*, subtitled "a partial account of the controversy over the authorship of Shakespeare's plays", is a short, lively, and scholarly story, helpfully illustrated by full-page plates. The author writes that "the purpose of this brief survey is not to argue the merits of either side". His humorous dedication, "To R.N.W.—who knows who wrote this", indicates a sufficient detachment.

Mr. Calvin Hoffman went to the lengths of persuading the Church authorities to allow him to peer into the graves of certain Elizabethan worthies, to be rewarded only with the sight of dust. Calvin Hoffman is a great protagonist of the claims of Christopher Marlowe to have written Shakespeare's plays, as he explained in his *The Man Who was Shakespeare*. This hypothesis is considered, along with the three other major claims—those of Bacon, the Oxford syndicate, and Lord Derby—by Dr. H. N. Gibson in his *The Shakespeare Claimants: a critical survey of the four principal theories concerning the authorship of the Shakespearean plays.* The judicious phraseology of the sub-title indicates the care which Dr. Gibson takes not to offend the protagonists of the claimants, nor to prejudice the issue.

CHAPTER 3

Shakespeare's Theatre and Productions

GRAHAM GREENE writes in his little book *British Dramatists*, in the Britain in Pictures series:

> Then in 1576 came the blow which looked like attaching playwrights permanently to the household, when the Corporation of London forbade the performance of plays in public within the bounds, for the sake of morality and hygiene. But this was answered in the same year with the first theatre, in Shoreditch, outside the city limits, and so for the first time we get the fixed stage, the management, the responsibility towards an audience, the profit-and-loss account—all those considerations which the dilettante regards as unseemly checks on the freedom of the artist, but which the artist knows to be the very mould of his technique and the challenge to his imagination.

M. C. Bradbrook, in her *The Rise of the Common Player: a study of actor and society in Shakespeare's England*, reminds her readers that the springtime of a language comes but once, and the springtime for the English language was between the arrival of Christopher Marlowe in 1587 and the death of Shakespeare in 1616. Its greatest triumphs were in dramatic poetry, and this poetry was not a book-art:

> By a 'play' it is probable that no Elizabethan would have meant the script or "book", but always an *event*, the play-in-being, the enacted mime in which players and audience shared. This deep and natural immersion in performance, this assumption of a common activity, was their most precious inheritance from the theatre of the Middle Ages.

But, as this book makes clear, the player had no recognized place in society. All men were expected to owe allegiance to a lord or master who could supervise them and answer for them to his lord or master. Miss Bradbrook writes, "One actress of consummate skill appeared in Elizabethan England; the Queen herself.

In her relations with her people, by responsive quickness she created a part for both to play."

Sir Tyrone Guthrie, in remarks quoted by Leslie Hotson in his book *Shakespeare's Wooden O,* said:

> Shakespeare will always have to be butchered as long as his work has to be produced in a sort of theatre for which the plays were not written, to which they are positively ill-adapted; a sort of theatre designed for effects which are irrelevant to Shakespeare's purpose, and inimical to the kind of effects which he sought.

Or, as Marshall McLuhan would say, the medium is the message.

Leslie Hotson quotes two dicta of William Poel, founder of the Elizabethan Stage Society in 1895 and author of *Shakespeare in the Theatre,* who first worked to restore Elizabethan plays to their proper setting: "Shakespeare invented his dramatic construction to suit his own particular stage"; "The plays were shaped to suit the theatre of the day and no other."

In his book Mr. Hotson goes to immense lengths to reconstruct for the reader exactly what the Shakespearean theatre was like. He has unearthed not only dimensions and plans, but also philosophic reasons why the Elizabethans produced "in the round" and much evidence to prove that this fact was obscured for two centuries by our Italianite preconceptions, which spoiled our own native English insights, the natural genius of this island. One can be in no doubt after reading this book, with its details taken from carpenters' bills of the year 1590 preserved in the Office of Works, of the sight, sound, smell, and feel of the wooden O.

Shakespeare's Globe Playhouse: a modern reconstruction in text and scale drawings by Irwin Smith, is based on the reconstruction of the Globe described in John Cranford Adams's book *The Globe Playhouse: its design and equipment.* After the publication of this book Irwin Smith and Dr. Adams built a scale model of the Globe Playhouse which is now on exhibition in the Folger Shakespeare Library in Washington. Irwin Smith cites the evidence upon which Dr. Adams based his reconstruction, using scale drawings, giving dimensions and positions for every individual piece of material used in the building. There are fifteen scale drawings printed in the book, and appendixes print copies of the builder's contracts. There is also a bibliography listing about ninety items for the reader who wishes to pursue the subject further. There are 16 plates reproducing maps and drawings of the sixteenth and seventeenth century, of London, Southwark and Bankside, and 9 other illustrations reproducing contemporary drawings of the inside of the theatres of the time. A final set of plates consists of photographs of the modern reconstruction of the Globe Theatre. The chapters of the book describe the site and shape of the Globe and then discuss in detail the dimensions, the fabric, the auditorium, the platform, the tiring-house, the inner stages, the rear stage, the second-level stages, the music gallery, and the superstructure. Then comes a most interesting attempt to "indicate some of the ways in which a study of original staging may throw light upon the dramatist's intent", by reconstructing, scene by scene, the presentation of *Romeo and Juliet* and *Henry IV, Part 2*;

> Because both plays utilize the resources of the multiple stage fully and with unusual freedom, because both contain scenes which are and deserve to be the subject of debate, and because both have sequences of scenes whose treatment in modern texts undoubtedly violate Shakespeare's design with respect to their staging.

Another splendid book, though not for the beginner, is Glynne Wickham's 2-volume *Early English Stages, 1300–1660*. The second volume covers the Shakespearean period. There is a very clearly drawn map of the city of London, *c.* 1600, which marks the sites of all the theatres. The first chapter asks and effectively answers the question: "Where did so startlingly original an idea as the Globe style of Playhouse spring from, and why did it appear at this particular moment of time?" There is also a good chapter on stage furniture and another on the emblematic tradition. A classified bibliography of the subject is promised for a third volume in the series which has yet to appear.

Bernard Beckerman's compact study entitled *Shakespeare at the Globe, 1599–1609*, considers the repertory, the dramaturgy, the stage, the acting, the staging, and the style. The first volume of *Shakespeare Survey* contains some scholarly articles on the Elizabethan stage. One is an account of the developments in the study of the subject since 1900 by Allardyce Nicoll, veteran historian of the theatre. John Dover Wilson writes on the production of *Titus Andronicus* in 1595; I. A. Shapiro has an essay on the Bankside theatres, illustrated with early engravings which he describes with care. G. E. Bentley writes on 'Shakespeare and the Blackfriars theatre'.

A. M. Nagler's *Shakespeare's Stage* is a good introduction to the subject. Although closely reasoned with many references to all the relevant authorities, its text flows with the readability of a narrative. It sets out to describe the theatre in which and with which Shakespeare had to work, and the author reminds us that Shakespeare "lived in the finest harmony with his audience", as is evident from the Prologue to *King Henry VIII*:

> I come no more to make you laugh: things now
> That bear a weighty and a serious brow,
> Sad, high and working, full of state and woe,
> Such noble scenes as draw the eye to flow,
> We now present. Those that can pity, here
> May, if they think it well, let fall a tear;
> The subject will deserve it. Such as give
> Their money out of hope they may believe,
> May here find truth too. Those that come to see
> Only a show or two, and so agree
> The play may pass, if they be still and willing,
> I'll undertake may see away their shilling
> Richly in two short hours. Only they
> That come to hear a merry bawdy play,
> A noise of targets, or to see a fellow
> In a long motley coat guarded with yellow,
> Will be deceived; for, gentle hearers, know,
> To rank our chosen truth with such a show
> As fool and fight is, beside forfeiting
> Our own brains, and the opinion that we bring,
> To make that only true we now intend,
> Will leave us never an understanding friend.
> Therefore, for goodness' sake, and as you are known
> The first and happiest hearers of the town,
> Be sad, as we would make ye: think ye see
> The very persons of our noble story
> As they were living; think you see them great,
> And follow'd with the general throng and sweat

Of thousand friends; then, in a moment, see
How soon this mightiness meets misery;
And if you can be merry then I'll say
A man may weep upon his wedding-day.

In this book, too, there is an appendix which sets out the history of the sketch by Johannes de Witt of the interior of the Swan Playhouse, and of a less well-known engraving, *The View of the Cittye of London from the North Towards the South*, which includes the only known contemporary view of the outside of the Curtain Theatre.

Key works on the study of the Elizabethan theatre are the 2 volumes edited by W. W. Greg from the documents deposited in the Library of Dulwich College, *Henslowe's Diary* and *Henslowe Papers*. Philip Henslowe was the business partner of Edward Alleyn, and together they built the Fortune Theatre in 1600 and drew up an agreement with the builder, who had been responsible for erecting the Globe Theatre the year before. This agreement has survived and is also reprinted in full in G. B. Harrison's book *Introducing Shakespeare*. The *Diary* runs from 1592 to 1603 and records the names of the plays performed in his theatre and companies who put them on as well as a financial account of the monies Henslowe received, which was one half of the gallery takings. After 1597, Henslowe became the banker for the Admiral's Men and records the advances he made for the purchase of plays and to the players themselves. He also financed the costuming and buying of properties. Among the Henslowe *Papers* is an inventory of the properties belonging to the Admiral's Company in 1598, which is also printed in Harrison's *Introducing Shakespeare*. These include some puzzling items, such as 'Hell's mouth' and 'City of Rome' as well as more recognizable items like 'Kent's wooden leg' and 'Mercury's wings'.

Ivor Brown, in his *How Shakespeare Spent the Day*, provides a popular account of the life of a theatrical company of those days, including a look at financial and medical matters. T. W. Baldwin's *The Organisation and Personnel of the Shakespearean Company* sets out the laws, customs, membership, and history of the Shakespearean company; dealing with the Shakespearean "clan", with finance, division of labour, apprenticeship, hired men, and the bookkeepers and their manuscripts. G. B. Harrison's *Elizabethan Plays and Players* and *Shakespeare at Work*, and William Bliss's *The Real Shakespeare*, are valuable. Another popular book, illustrated from contemporary prints with appendixes giving transcripts of manuscripts, is a study by C. Walter Hodges of the Elizabethan theatre called *The Globe Restored*. Francis Berry's *The Shakespeare Inset: word and picture* may be regarded as a "fresh attack on the problem of the relation between language and spectacle in the dramatic poetry or poetic drama of Shakespeare", arguing that his plays are both poetry and action.

Much thought has been given by some writers to the question of the boy actors who played the women's parts in Shakespeare's day. A collection entitled *Papers mainly Shakespearean*, edited by G. I. Duthie, contains an essay on 'Shakespeare's celibate stage' with particular reference to *As You Like It, Antony and Cleopatra*, and *The Winter's Tale*.

W. Robertson Davies published a thorough and entertaining book on *Shakespeare's Boy Actors* in 1939 in which he asks, among other things, what effect the indecent dialogue was likely to have had on the boys; and also how the boys would have responded to the physical love-play that is a part of many of the scenes in such plays as *Romeo and Juliet*. His conclusion was that the boys would have taken it all in their stride, and that the audiences would have relished, as always, such intimacies, boys or not.

Dr. Jan Kott, in a volume entitled *Shakespeare Our Contemporary*, demonstrates that what he calls a "full ambiguity" between the sexes is created in such plays as *As You Like It* and *Twelfth Night* by boys acting the female roles. Dr. Kott has been impressed by the arguments of McLuhan on the breaking down of the "polarity between the sexes" in our day. He suggests that people are beginning to wear costume similar to that worn in the time of Elizabeth, likening the mini-skirted girl to the Elizabethan page. Thus, he argues, we can today better understand the characterization of Shakespeare's women.

FIG. 1. The gestures of actors of the seventeenth century—an illustration from Bulwer's *Chirologia*, London, 1644.

J. L. Styan, in his recent *Shakespeare's Stagecraft*, writes of the boy actors: "All the women have to play out their parts with warmth, and sometimes with coquetry. Kisses abound. For the sexual relationship is repeatedly Shakespeare's concern, and it is a Victorian myth that the boy actors were not centrally involved in a sexual situation . . . conveying sexual attractiveness was a condition of the boy player's art."

The audience of Shakespeare's day has been the subject of several studies, notably Professor Harbage's *Shakespeare's Audience* and A. C. Sprague's *Shakespeare and His Audience: a study in the technique of exposition*. Martin Holmes's *Shakespeare's Public: the touchstone of his genius* is another thorough study of this theme.

The great works of scholarship which opened men's eyes to the facts were E. K. Chambers's *Elizabethan Stage*, in 4 volumes, and its continuation, *The Jacobean and Caroline Stage* by G. E. Bentley and Hotson's *The Commonwealth and Restoration Stage*. Three other works, less frequently found on library shelves, slighter, but still very informative, are J. Q. Adams's *Shakespearean Playhouses*, which is a history from the beginnings to the Restoration; W. J. Lawrence's *Elizabethan Playhouse* in 2 volumes; and A. H. Thorndike's *Shakespeare's Theatre*.

Sir Walter Greg's *Dramatic Documents from the Elizabethan Playhouses: stage plots: actors' parts: prompt books* tells us "something at least of the conditions of performance, and something about the nature of the texts in use". He discusses three types of document, namely "the book" or authorized prompt copy; "parts" of the several characters; and the "plots" or skeleton outlines of the plays.

M. C. Bradbrook's *Elizabethan Stage Conditions: a study of their place in the interpretation of Shakespeare's plays* is all that it thereby claims to be. L. C. Knights, in his *Drama and Society in the Age of Jonson*, has a section on 'Shakespeare and profit inflations' which sets out to "suggest a few of the intercommunications between economic and social conditions and one [e.g. drama] of the cultural forms of the period"; this may seem a little remote from the problems of production, but sets them in their economic context.

Shakespeare Survey 12, edited by Allardyce Nicoll, is devoted to a consideration of Shakespeare production, most of the papers being on the Elizabethan stage—"the value of the study of Elizabethan stage conditions lies in this elucidation of the author's methods".

George C. D. Odell's 2 volumes on *Shakespeare from Betterton to Irving*, a long and detailed narrative, describes productions in which such actors as Garrick, Kemble, and Kean played the leading parts, and continues the story to the end of the nineteenth century.

A small pamphlet by Harold Child, *The Shakespeare Productions of John Philip Kemble* (who was first engaged by the company at Drury Lane in 1783) is a useful summary.

Alan S. Downer's *The Eminent Tragedian, William Charles Macready*, contains fine descriptions of the notable spectacles which Macready made of Shakespeare's plays in his career as actor and manager at Covent Garden and Drury Lane during the first half of the nineteenth century.

The more one reads about this subject the more is one convinced that only in the twentieth century has real justice been done to Shakespeare. Hazleton Spencer, in his *Shakespeare Improved: the Restoration versions in Quarto and on the stage*, merely proves the point that Shakespeare is best not improved, but presented as he intended. The story of how the twentieth-century producer slowly came to terms with Shakespeare is largely the story of the productions of William Poel and Harley Granville-Barker. Robert Speaight, himself an actor, has written a book for the Society of Theatre Research entitled *William Poel and the Elizabethan Revival*. In this he tells how Poel came to believe that Shakespeare the poet was "his own scene painter and electrician". This led him to devote his career to the presentation of Shakespeare's plays as they had been presented on the Elizabethan stage. Speaight's account is particularly vivid because he was himself involved with Poel in the latter part of his life. The book has a chronological list of the stage productions and other activities of Poel from 1878 to 1934. A list of his writings and of other people's writings about him is also included.

A chronological survey is presented by Gordon Crosse in his *Shakespearian Playgoing, 1890–1952,* which is illustrated from the Raymond Mander and Joe Mitchenson theatre collection.

The debt to Granville-Barker is acknowledged by J. L. Styan in his already-mentioned *Shakespeare's Stagecraft,* a splendidly vivid study, which is divided into four parts 'Shakespeare's theatre equipment', 'Shakespeare's visual craft', 'Shakespeare's aural craft' and 'Total theatre', the quotations from the plays which illustrate the argument being themselves a fascinating education in the use of words.

Alfred Harbage, in his small book *Theatre for Shakespeare,* writes: "Knowledge of the Elizabethan theatre and its methods is garnered in the hope that modern producers of Shakespeare will seek to apply it." W. Moelwyn Merchant's book *Shakespeare and the Artist* studies in large quarto pages, lavishly illustrated with full plate reproductions of the work of artists through the ages, and with stage settings of many great producers, what the author calls the "visual tradition" in the interpretation of Shakespeare. A. C. Sprague's two books, *Shakespeare and the Actors* and *Shakespearian Players and Performances,* trace the development of Shakespeare production with particular reference to the great acting traditions.

T. S. Eliot, in his *Elizabethan Essays,* wrote: "I want a direct relationship between the work of art and myself and I want the performance (of a play) to be such as will not interrupt or alter this relationship." Cecile de Banke's book *Shakespearean Stage Production Then and Now* gives ample data for the achievement of such a relationship. Her book is in 4 parts. The first considers the staging of the plays, comparing Elizabethan and Jacobean methods with modern, in stage settings, lighting, properties, and sound effects. The second is on actors and acting, with a summary of Shakespearean acting techniques for use on the modern stage. Part III is about costume, giving details of Elizabethan costume and some hints on creating these in a modern production. Part IV is on music and dancing, setting out the steps of Elizabethan dances, giving advice on Elizabethan music available today, and a list of recordings recommended for stage production. Throughout the author is trying to help the modern producer to achieve the conditions existing when the plays were first performed. As she says in her introduction, the amateur producer when seeking guidance from books is overwhelmed by the abundance available.

Therefore Cecile de Banke has attempted to provide in one book "the gathered facts and conjectures of the most outstanding Shakespeare scholars" so that the "scholar-player" may at leisure follow the trail for himself. She has set out in ample and well-annotated bibliographies details of the books she has drawn from. Ronald Watkins has attempted, in his *On Producing Shakespeare*, to explain why he thinks he knows the right way to produce Shakespeare. He acknowledges his debt to Harley Granville-Barker's *Prefaces to Shakespeare* and the work of two American scholars, J. C. Adams's *The Globe Playhouse: its design and equipment* and T. W. Baldwin's *The Organisation and Personnel of the Shakespearean Company*. Watkins says that "never since the closing of the theatres in 1642 has a play of his been performed in the conditions for which he devised it". The book's two principal chapters are 'The acting tradition of the Chamberlain's men' and 'The poet's stagecraft'. At the end, as a sort of tail-piece, is a chapter entitled 'Macbeth at the Globe' in which he takes his cue from Dr. Richard Flatter's statement in *Shakespeare's Producing Hand* that "the text of *Macbeth* is the only one of which we may assume with any measure of certainty that it shows no traces of 'editorial interference' and is the only play from which the real yard-stick of Shakespeare's diction can be obtained." G. Wilson Knight, with much experience as a producer of Shakespeare with the Toronto Shakespeare Society, also has a chapter on the production of *Macbeth*, entitled 'The Ideal Production' in his book *Principles of Shakespearean Production: with especial reference to the tragedies*.

Nevill Coghill, in his *Shakespeare's Professional Skills*, provides some valuable material for the producer. He writes:

> My starting point is how to tell a story on the stage, and this was also Shakespeare's primal starting point, so far as one can tell; for he ransacked history and fiction for stories that could be made significant and told, or re-told, upon a stage. He was a supreme stage-story-teller and perceived that the basic source of all meaning that can be presented through this medium was the image of a human action.

This book also has a chapter of interest to the textual critics, entitled 'Revision after performance' of which he writes:

> This chapter will offer a dramaturgical analysis of certain passages in the 1623 Folio text of *Othello* which diverge from the 1622 Quarto text, and will show that these divergencies can only be explained on the supposition that, in this play at least, Folio embodies a Shakespearean revision of the play that appears in the Quarto. As this conclusion is directly contrary to the most recent findings of textual criticism, the chapter will begin with a study of received opinion.

John Russell Brown, in his *Shakespeare's Plays in Performance*, advocates a decisive move away from literary criticism towards a study of the performance of the plays. He writes:

> I start with the text and the actor, which is the closest point of contact between Shakespeare and those who perform his plays. Problems of style and interpretation are at once encountered, and confusions due to changes in taste and conditions of performance. While general considerations prepare for the more particular, every chapter in the first part of the book is basically concerned with how an actor must respond to the text and what revaluations of that text are accomplished by his performance.

He quotes Gordon Craig's *On the Art of Theatre* with approval: "Let me tell you at the commencement that it is the large and sweeping impression produced by means of scene and the movement of the figures which is the most valuable means at your disposal", and he explains what stage effects are required by the dialogue. The last part of the book is about some modern productions of Shakespeare, beginning with Zeffirelli's *Romeo and Juliet* and continuing with some of the Royal Shakespeare Company's productions and an account of Olivier's *Othello*, concluding with a survey of productions of *Twelfth Night*. The powerful impact on the public of Zeffirelli's film version of *The Taming of the Shrew*, which is 2 hours of the sheerest enjoyment imaginable, must strengthen the hand of those who, like Dr. Brown, demand a Shakespeare in the theatre, not in the study, and confirms the eclipse of those who follow Charles Lamb, who held the plays were not actable, or those who profess not to be able to withstand the mangling of their sensibilities when they see the plays acted.

Anne Righter, in her *Shakespeare and the Idea of the Play*, also studies Shakespeare as a practising dramatist in relation to the dramatic ideas of the sixteenth century and the relationship that existed between the actors and the audiences in Elizabethan times. She argues that Shakespeare finally developed a dislike of the theatre, a conclusion that will not be popular.

J. C. Trewin, in his *Shakespeare on the English Stage, 1900–1964*, subtitled 'A survey of productions illustrated from the Raymond Mander and Joe Mitchenson theatre collection', has attempted a monumental task to trace the evolution of understanding in the production of Shakespeare during these last 60 years. The book begins with Irving as Coriolanus and ends with Paul Scofield as Lear. The book has some useful appendixes; one listing West End productions from 1900 to 1964, including theatres not strictly in the West End, such as the Lyric, Hammersmith; the second listing productions at the Old Vic, 1914–64; and the third those at Stratford 1879–1964. There is also a 7-page short-title bibliography of books relating to Shakespeare production, including many by actors and actresses, and some by notable producers such as Komisarjevsky's famous *Myself and the Theatre*. J. C. Trewin has himself produced another book of theatrical records, *The Birmingham Repertory Theatre, 1913–1963*, of great value to the student of Shakespearean productions. C. B. Hogans's *Shakespeare in the Theatre* is an erudite 2-volume work, giving a detailed record of all performances in London, 1701–1800, that is casts and receipts, but no dramatic criticism. Here should be mentioned an unpretentious but useful collection of dramatic criticism by Herbert Farjeon, entitled *The Shakespearean Scene*. Thirty-one of the plays are reviewed in performances that took place between 1920 and 1940. The story of the Old Vic and Sadlers Wells, *A Theatre for Everybody* by Edward J. Dent, has a chapter on Shakespeare productions. Dent claims that "the history of Shakespeare representation and Shakespeare appreciation is the history of the English theatre and the history of English manners, taste and culture as well".

Of great interest is Mikhail M. Morozov's short account published in 1947 of *Shakespeare and the Soviet Stage.* Professor Dover Wilson writes in his introduction to this book:

> Time and again I have been struck with the similarity, even sometimes the simultaneity, of response to this or that aspect of Shakespeare in the two countries. *King Lear*, the popularity of which is very great in the U.S.S.R., was first revealed in its true greatness by Solomon Mikhoels of the State Jewish Theatre, while it has quite recently been discovered as a great *acting* play in Britain, after being virtually banished from the stage for a century by Charles Lamb's dictum that 'The Lear of Shakespeare cannot be acted'.

The performance during the Festival of Britain in 1951 of the tetralogy of historical plays, *Richard II, Henry IV, Parts 1 and 2,* and *Henry V,* produced by Michael Redgrave, John Kidd, and Anthony Quayle, was commemorated by a volume edited by John Dover Wilson and T. C. Worsley. Apart from the evocative illustrations, the book is valuable for the descriptions of the productions by Mr. Worsley and for the detailed list of the cast in each of the four productions.

Albums of photographs of theatrical productions are much loved by the theatre-goer. For the Shakespearean none are to be more recommended than the succession of volumes recording successive seasons at the Old Vic, entitled *Shakespeare at the Old Vic*, compiled and written by Mary Clarke and illustrated by photographs by such great exponents of the art as Angus McBean, Tony Armstrong Jones, Houston Rogers, and David Sim. The volumes cover the 5-year plan of the Old Vic during which all the plays in the First Folio were produced.

Another very fine album is that of the *Royal Shakespeare Theatre Company, 1960–63*, recording performances in Stratford-on-Avon and London directed by Peter Hall, whose work has been so notable. The album contains a catena of news items, editorials, and notices of key productions, and a fascinating essay by Robert Bolt entitled 'Shakespeare and the modern playwright'.

Two most exciting contributions to the study of Shakespeare production in recent years are the books in which Tyrone Guthrie describes the Shakespeare Festivals held at Stratford, Ontario, in 1953 and 1954. The first is entitled *Renown at Stratford* and the second *Twice Have the Trumpets Sounded*. The story of the organization of these festivals, which originally were the brain children of a businessman, Tom Patterson, is itself fascinating. Tyrone Guthrie illuminates his narrative with insights into the problems of a Canadian production. No manufacturer could be found whose mass production methods could cope with an order for forty pairs of shoes for *Richard III*. These had to be made, and were made very competently, by an old Jewish craftsman whose hands and eyes in this machine age had not lost their cunning. Likewise a Czech made the boots required in *All's Well That Ends Well*. Grant Macdonald contributes numerous drawings and paintings of the actors and actresses in their costumes.

No one who has seen Zeffirelli's film production of *The Taming of the Shrew* can possibly doubt that the cinema has only just begun to make the most of the unlimited dramatic possibilities of Shakespeare's plays. The magnificent visual experience which this film presents, its muted colour and medieval contrasts dominating the verse, but never contradicting it, so that the poetic movement of the camera is stilled to listen to the words of the dramatist, is sheer enjoyment. The interest is in the acting; in the mime and the movement of the facial muscles, the gestures of body and limb—and this is surely as Shakespeare would have wished. A short account of *Shakespeare in Film, Radio and Television* by John Russell Taylor is included in *Shakespeare: a celebration, 1564–1964* edited by T. J. B. Spencer, in which the reader is reminded of great films: Orson Welles as Macbeth; Olivier as Hamlet, Henry V, and Richard III; and the epoch-making *Age of Kings* sequence on B.B.C. Television. Taylor makes many reservations about the performance of Shakespeare in the new mass media. It is plain that the production of Shakespeare on T.V. or on the wide screen is a new challenge—as, for instance, the recent *Othello* of Olivier, translated from stage to screen with entire success.

Recordings of Shakespeare plays on tape and long-playing records are also valuable sources of enlightenment. Suffice it to mention here a series of recordings, by the Globe Shakespeare Company, under the directorship of Dr. Bertram L. Joseph, whose book, *Acting Shakespeare*, is full of practical ideas. These recordings are designed to provide teachers and students with performances in which the actor thinks clearly the sense of every word he utters, and thus provides the listener with a dramatic experience of some freshness and immediacy. The recordings are sold together with a booklet, prepared by Dr. Joseph, which contains a commentary and explanations clarifying difficulties likely to be encountered by a modern listener to the Elizabethan language.

Two other practical books on the production of the plays are Guy Boas's *Shakespeare and the Young Actor: a guide to production*, the author being Headmaster, Sloane School, Chelsea, at the time he wrote the book, and C. B. Purdom's *Producing Shakespeare*, written also out of much experience. Mr. Purdom has followed up this book with another, *What Happens in Shakespeare*, which is an explanation of Shakespeare's dramatic methods, with valuable advice to the actor on the speaking of his verse so as to achieve the desired interpretation of Shakespeare's intentions.

Another line of research is suggested by Toby Lelyveld in his *Shylock on the Stage*, a study of the stage history of the *Merchant of Venice* from the seventeenth century to the present, with a useful bibliography.

CHAPTER 4

The Text of Shakespeare's Works

"TRY to read Shakespeare in the . . . facsimile of the First Folio, and you will be held up in almost every line by misprints, or unintelligible punctuation, or mislining of the verse, or missing stage directions, to say nothing of the old spelling and a dozen other puzzling features. It took two and a half centuries of editing to convert that mass of perplexities to the 'Globe Shakespeare' of today." Thus wrote Professor J. Dover Wilson in the first of his articles, 'The new way with Shakespeare's texts: an introduction for lay readers', which appeared in the seventh volume of *Shakespeare Survey*. This essay is the best short introduction I know to what Wilson calls the "revolution" in Shakespeare textual criticism which was initiated in 1892 by the foundation of the London Bibliographical Society. "The chief moving spirit" of this work was Alfred Pollard, at that time in charge of the Antiquarian side of the Department of Printed Books at the British Museum. Ronald B. McKerrow and Walter W. Greg joined Pollard in his labours. Greg published an edition of *Henslowe's Diary* and of the *Henslowe Papers*, thus collecting the most reliable information available about the Elizabethan theatre. His work was followed up by an official of the Board of Education, E. K. Chambers, in his 4-volume study of *The Elizabethan Stage*, published in 1923. Pollard, Greg, and McKerrow made the British Museum the world's foremost centre of Elizabethan studies. McKerrow published in 1910 an epoch-making edition of the works of Thomas Nashe, but it was not until 1939 that he was able to publish his *Prolegomena for the Oxford Shakespeare*. But he died in 1940, and his edition of Shakespeare's works was lost to the world. He writes in his *Prolegomena*:

> Truth is truth and logic is logic, whether we are writing of the phenomena of gravitation or of the sources of a line of poetry and in a sense any honestly conducted enquiry may be termed scientific; but the man of science, as science is usually understood, who builds up his theories on the basis of a series of propositions the truth of each of which can be demonstrated by experiments capable of repetition whenever desired, in circumstances which so far as their influence on the results obtained is concerned are identical, is in a position to arrive at a very different order of certainty from the textual critic, to whom experiment is as a rule impossible . . . his arguments . . . based on what seem to him, from "his knowledge of human nature" and from what he can learn of the procedure and habits of early copyists, printers, and theatrical producers, most likely to have occurred, and which can seldom or never be more than *probably* correct, even though the probability may in some cases be of a high degree.

Greg wrote in his memoir of McKerrow that he had insisted on "the general principle of making the last edition that seems to have been corrected by the author the foundation of the text". This edition he called the "copy-text" and his *Prolegomena* consists of 3 parts: I, the basis of a reprint; II, the degree of exactitude to be aimed at in reproducing the copy-text; and III, the recording of the readings of other editions than the copy-text.

Sir Walter Greg, in his *The Editorial Problem in Shakespeare: a survey of the foundations of the text*, pays tribute to his friend and colleague, but wishes to modify his rules which he considers too rigid. He writes in his first chapter, which he entitles 'A prolegomena—on editing Shakespeare': "I have done no more than extract from McKerrow's discussion the formal rules that, as I understand, were to govern his own procedure, and elaborate or modify them in such manner as appeared to me desirable."

There is an Old Testament quality about these truly great scholars as they wrestled with the immense problems of arriving at a text which would be as near as possible to that written by Shakespeare in the prompt copies from which his plays were produced. How grateful the poet would be to these men, striving to rescue his work from the distorting influence of time, which he so much feared. Oddly enough, there is no great discussion by them about Shakespeare's failure to see his plays through the press. It is well here to recall the words of Heminge and Condell in their preface to the First Folio:

> It had been a thing, we confess, worthy to have been wished that the author himself had lived to have set forth and oversee his own writings. But since it hath been ordained otherwise, and he by death departed from that right, we pray you do not envy his friends the office of their care and pain to have collected and published them; and so to have published them as where before you were abused with divers stolen and surreptitious copies, maimed and deformed by the frauds and stealths of injurious impostors that exposed them, even those are now offered to your view cured and perfect of their limbs; and all the rest absolute in their numbers as he conceived them. Who, as he was a happy imitator of nature, was a most gentle expressor of it. His mind and hand went together; and what he thought, he uttered with that easiness that we have scarce received from him a blot in his papers.

How far they were from succeeding in their task the first paragraph of this chapter indicates, yet they did their best.

W. W. Greg has published a very considerable study of the First Folio, entitled *Shakespeare's First Folio: its bibliographical and textual history*, of which he writes:

> All I have tried to do is to set out the evidence and summarise on each point under discussion the view now generally held by scholars, or, if there is no commonly accepted opinion, the view that seems in best accord with the evidence. I am, of course, perfectly aware that this only means that I have expressed the view with which I personally agree; but I have endeavoured to be as objective as possible.

He also says that "it would be foolish to suppose that Shakespeare was indifferent to the fate of his own works. The mere length of some of his plays, of *Hamlet*, of *Richard III*, of *Coriolanus*, for example, must have made it difficult to produce them in their entirety on the stage, and suggests that he had an alternative mode of publication in view." Greg's work on the First Folio is organized in four main sections; first 'Planning the collection' then 'Question of copyright' followed by the main body of the book in 3 parts 'Editorial problems' and finally 'The printing'. A new study of the First Folio, highly commended by Greg, is Dr. Alice Walker's *Textual Problems of the First Folio*. A recently published, close study of the mechanics of the printing in the 1620's is C. K. Hinman's *The Printing and Proof Reading of the First Folio of*

Shakespeare. The collating machine that C. K. Hinman used to check the seventy copies of the *First Folio* in the Folger Library has by a strange sequence of events come to rest in the Library of Edinburgh University, where the ingenious arrangement of mirrors and lights can be seen by those who wish to delve into the technology of bibliography. Another book, also recently published, that describes the way in which the First Folio was printed, is Kenneth Hardacre's *Shakespeare's Printers*.

A map of the whole territory within which these textual and exegetical struggles are carried on, is provided by Greg's famous *Bibliography of the English Printed Drama to the Restoration* and by Bartlett and Pollard's *Census of Shakespeare Plays in Quarto, 1594–1709*.

Fredson Bowers is perhaps the foremost exponent of the science of the "new bibliography", and he presents an explanation of principles and methods in his Rosenbach fellowship lectures published under the title *On Editing Shakespeare and the Elizabethan Dramatists*. He writes:

> My intent is not to offer a textbook for editors; rather, by discussion to attempt to clear the ground, to fix certain concepts; and, by a survey of the peculiar problems that arise in the editing of Shakespeare and his fellow dramatists, to illustrate how the basic methods for tackling these problems stem from a few necessary principles which alone give these methods their reason.

Bowers thinks there is years of drudgery in store for the young scholars if they are going to establish a definitive text for Shakespeare's plays. E. A. J. Honigmann's *The Stability of Shakespeare's Text*, discusses the work of the bibliographers from Greg, McKerrow, and Pollard, through J. D. Wilson's *The Manuscript of Shakespeare's Hamlet* to Alice Walker and Fredson Bowers. He comes to pessimistic conclusions; even that perhaps a definitive text will never be possible. Honigmann's book is written with an effort not to be too technical in this most technical field.

A. W. Pollard's entertaining *Shakespeare's Fight with the Pirates and the Problem of the Transmission of his Text* describes the economics of the printing trade in Shakespeare's day and disposes of the view that all the plays published in quarto editions were

TWELFTH-NIGHT;

O R,

What you will.

A C T I. S C E N E I.

S C E N E I. *The Palace.*

Enter the Duke, Curio, *and Lords.*

D U K E.

F Mufick be the Food of Love, play on,
Give me excefs of it; that furfeiting
The Appetite may ficken, and fo die.
That Strain again, it had a dying Fall:
O, it came o'er my Ear, like the fweet Wind
That breathes upon a Bank of Violets,
Stealing, and giving Odour. Enough, no more;
'Tis not fo fweet now, as it was before.
O Spirit of Love, how quick and frefh art thou!
That notwithftanding thy Capacity,
Recciveth as the Sea; Nought enters there,
Of what validity and pitch fo e'er,
But falls into Abatement, and low Price,
Even in a Minute; fo full of Shapes is Fancy,
That it alone is high fantaftical.
　Cur. Will you go hunt, my Lord?
　Duke. What, *Curio?*

　　　　　　　A a 3　　　　　　　　　　　*Cur.*

FIG. 2. Format of former days—how Shakespeare has been read in the
past. I—In the edition of Nicholas Rowe, 1709.

PRINCE OF DENMARK.   69

And, by oppofing, end them?—To die,—to fleep,—
No more;—and, by a fleep, to fay we end
The heart-ach, and the thoufand natural fhocks
That flefh is heir to,—'tis a confummation
Devoutly to be wifh'd.   To die;—to fleep;—
To fleep! perchance, to dream;—ay, there's the rub;
For in that fleep of death what dreams may come,
When we have fhuffled off this mortal coil[2],
Muft give us paufe: There's the refpect,[3]
That makes calamity of fo long life:
For who would bear the whips and fcorns of time[4],
The oppreffor's wrong, the proud man's contumely[5],
The pangs of defpis'd love, the law's delay,
The infolence of office, and the fpurns
That patient merit of the unworthy takes,
When he himfelf might his quietus make
With a bare bodkin[6]? who would fardels bear,
To grunt and fweat under a weary life;
But that the dread of fomething after death,—

           U 6   The

    I know not why there fhould be fo much folicitude about this meta-phor. Shakfpeare breaks his metaphors often, and in this defultory fpeech there was lefs need of preferving them. JOHNSON.

    [2] i. e. turmoil, buftle.

    [3] i. e. the confideration.

    [4] The evils here complained of are not the product of time or duration fimply, but of a corrupted age or manners. We may be fure, then, that Shakfpeare wrote
       — *the whips and fcorns* of th' *time*.
And the defcription of the evils of a corrupt age, which follows, confirms this emendation. WARBURTON.

    It may be remarked, that Hamlet, in his enumeration of miferies, forgets, whether properly or not, that he is a prince, and mentions many evils to which inferior ftations are expofed. JOHNSON.

    [5] Thus the quarto. The folio reads—the *poor* man's contumely; the contumely which the poor man is obliged to endure.
       'Nil habet infelix paupertas durius in fe,
       " Quam quod ridiculos homines facit."

    [6] The firft expreffion probably alluded to the writ of difcharge, which was formerly granted to thofe barons and knights who perfonally attended the king on any foreign expedition, and were therefore exempted from the claims of fcutage, or a tax on every knights fee. This difcharge was called a *quietus*.
    It is at this time the term for the acquittance which every fheriff receives on fettling his accounts at the exchequer.

FIG. 3. Format of former days. II—In the edition of Edmond Malone, 1786.

I prithee, when thou seest that act afoot,
Even with the very comment of thy soul
Observe mine uncle: if his occulted guilt
Do not itself unkennel in one speech,
It is a damned ghost that we have seen,
And my imaginations are as foul
As Vulcan's stithy. Give him heedful note;
For I mine eyes will rivet to his face,   90
And after we will both our judgements join
In censure of his seeming.

Hor.   Well, my lord:
If he steal aught the whilst this play is playing,
And 'scape detecting, I will pay the theft.

Ham. They are coming to the play; I must
be idle:
Get you a place.

Danish march. A flourish. Enter KING, QUEEN,
POLONIUS, OPHELIA, ROSENCRANTZ, GUILD-
ENSTERN, *and others.*

King. How fares our cousin Hamlet?

Ham. Excellent, i' faith; of the chameleon's
dish: I eat the air, promise-crammed: you cannot feed capons so.   100

King. I have nothing with this answer, Hamlet; these words are not mine.

Ham. No, nor mine now. [*To Polonius*] My
lord, you played once i' the university, you say?

Pol. That did I, my lord; and was accounted
a good actor.

Ham. What did you enact?

Pol. I did enact Julius Cæsar: I was killed
i' the Capitol; Brutus killed me.

Ham. It was a brute part of him to kill so
capital a calf there. Be the players ready? 111

Ros. Ay, my lord; they stay upon your patience.

Queen. Come hither, my dear Hamlet, sit by
me.

Ham. No, good mother, here's metal more
attractive.

Pol. [*To the King*] O, ho! do you mark that?

Ham. Lady, shall I lie in your lap?
                    [*Lying down at Ophelia's feet.*

Oph. No, my lord.   120

Ham. I mean, my head upon your lap?

Oph. Ay, my lord.

Ham. Do you think I meant country matters?

Oph. I think nothing, my lord.

Ham. That's a fair thought to lie between
maids' legs.

Oph. What is, my lord?

Ham. Nothing.

Oph. You are merry, my lord.

Ham. Who, I?

Oph. Ay, my lord.   130

Ham. O God, your only jig-maker. What
should a man do but be merry? for, look you,
how cheerfully my mother looks, and my father
died within these two hours.

Oph. Nay, 'tis twice two months, my lord.

Ham. So long? Nay then, let the devil wear
black, for I'll have a suit of sables. O heavens!
die two months ago, and not forgotten yet?
Then there's hope a great man's memory may
outlive his life half a year: but, by'r lady, he
must build churches, then; or else shall he suffer
not thinking on, with the hobby-horse, whose

epitaph is 'For, O, for, O, the hobby-horse is
forgot.'

Hautboys play. The dumb-show enters.

Enter a King *and a* Queen *very lovingly; the*
Queen *embracing him, and he her. She
kneels, and makes show of protestation unto
him. He takes her up, and declines his head
upon her neck: lays him down upon a bank of
flowers: she, seeing him asleep, leaves him.
Anon comes in a fellow, takes off his crown,
kisses it, and pours poison in the* King's *ears,
and exit. The* Queen *returns; finds the*
King *dead, and makes passionate action. The*
Poisoner, *with some two or three* Mutes,
*comes in again, seeming to lament with her.
The dead body is carried away. The* Poisoner
wooes the Queen *with gifts: she seems loath
and unwilling awhile, but in the end accepts
his love.*   [*Exeunt.*

Oph. What means this, my lord?

Ham. Marry, this is miching mallecho; it
means mischief.

Oph. Belike this show imports the argument
of the play.   150

Enter Prologue.

Ham. We shall know by this fellow: the
players cannot keep counsel; they'll tell all.

Oph. Will he tell us what this show meant?

Ham. Ay, or any show that you'll show him:
be not you ashamed to show, he'll not shame to
tell you what it means.

Oph. You are naught, you are naught: I'll
mark the play.

Pro. For us, and for our tragedy,
            Here stooping to your clemency,   160
            We beg your hearing patiently. [*Exit.*

Ham. Is this a prologue, or the posy of a ring?

Oph. 'Tis brief, my lord.

Ham. As woman's love.

Enter two Players, King *and* Queen.

P. King. Full thirty times hath Phœbus'
            cart gone round
Neptune's salt wash and Tellus' orbed ground,
And thirty dozen moons with borrow'd sheen
About the world have times twelve thirties been.
Since love our hearts and Hymen did our hands
Unite commutual in most sacred bands.   170

P. Queen. So many journeys may the sun
            and moon
Make us again count o'er ere love be done!
But, woe is me, you are so sick of late,
So far from cheer and from your former state,
That I distrust you. Yet, though I distrust,
Discomfort you, my lord, it nothing must:
For women's fear and love holds quantity;
In neither aught, or in extremity.
Now, what my love is, proof hath made you
            know:
And as my love is sized, my fear is so: 180
Where love is great, the littlest doubts are fear;
Where little fears grow great, great love grows
            there.

P. King. 'Faith, I must leave thee, love,
            and shortly too:
My operant powers their functions leave to do:

FIG. 4. Format of former days. III—In the Globe edition of W. G.
Clark and W. A. Wright, 1864.

King.   O, 'tis too true! how smart
A lash that speech doth give my conscience!
The harlot's cheek, beautied with plast'ring art,
Is not more ugly to the thing that helps it,
Than is my deed to my most painted word:
O heavy burden!   [*Aside.*
Pol. I hear him coming; let's withdraw, my
lord.   [*Exeunt* KING *and* POL.

Enter HAMLET.

Ham. To be, or not to be, that is the ques-
tion:—
Whether 'tis nobler in the mind to suffer
The slings and arrows of outrageous fortune ;
Or to take arms against a sea of troubles,
And, by opposing, end them?—To die,—to
sleep,—
No more ;—and, by a sleep, to say we end
The heart-ache, and the thousand natural shocks
That flesh is heir to,—'tis a consummation
Devoutly to be wish'd. To die ;—to sleep ;—
To sleep! perchance to dream ;—ay, there's the
rub ;
For in that sleep of death what dreams may come,
When we have shuffled off this mortal coil,*
Must give us pause : There's the respect†
That makes calamity of so long life :
For who would bear the whips and scorns of time,
The oppressor's wrong, the proud man's con-
tumely,‡
The pangs of despis'd love, the law's delay,
The insolence of office, and the spurns
That patient merit of the unworthy takes,
When he himself might his quietus§ make
With a bare bodkin? ‖ who would fardels ¶ bear,
To grunt and sweat under a weary life ;
But that the dread of something after death,—
The undiscover'd country, from whose bourn**
No traveller returns, puzzles the will ;
And makes us rather bear those ills we have,
Than fly to others that we know not of†
Thus conscience does make cowards of us all ;
And thus the native hue of resolution
Is sicklied o'er with the pale cast of thought ;
And enterprizes of great pith and moment,
With this regard, their currents turn awry,
And lose the name of action.—Soft you, now !
The fair Ophelia :—Nymph, in thy orisons ††
Be all my sins remember'd.
Oph.   Good my lord,
How does your honour for this many a day?
Ham. I humbly thank you ; well.
Oph. My lord, I have remembrances of yours,
That I have longed long to re-deliver ;
I pray you, now receive them.
Ham.   No, not I ;
I never gave you aught.
Oph. My honour'd lord, you know right well
you did ;
And, with them, words of so weet breath com-
pos'd :
As made the things more rich : their perfume lost,
Take these again ; for to the noble mind,
Rich gifts wax poor when givers prove unkind.
There, my lord.
Ham. Ha, ha! are you honest?
Oph. My lord?
Ham. Are you fair?
Oph. What means your lordship?
Ham. That if you be honest and fair, your

* Stir, bustle.
+ Consideration.   ‡ Rudeness.   § Quiet.
‖ The ancient term for a small dagger.
¶ Pack, burden.   ** Boundary, limits.
†† Prayers.   ‡‡ Alienation of mind.
B

honesty should admit no discourse to your
beauty.
Oph. Could beauty, my lord, have better com-
merce than with honesty?
Ham. Ay, truly; for the power of beauty will
sooner debase honesty from what it is than the
force of honesty can translate beauty into his
likeness ; this was sometime a paradox, but now
the time gives it proof. I did love you once.
Oph. Indeed, my lord, you made me believe so.
Ham. You should not have believed me : for
virtue cannot so inoculate our old stock, but we
shall relish of it : I loved you not.
Oph. I was the more deceived.
Ham. Get thee to a nunnery; Why would'st
thou be a breeder of sinners? I am myself indifferent honest; but yet I could accuse me of
such things, that it were better my mother had
not borne me : I am very proud, revengeful,
ambitious ; with more offences at my beck than
I have thoughts to put them in, imagination to
give them shape, or 'time to act them in.
What should such fellows as I do crawling
between earth and heaven! We are arrant knaves,
all ; believe none of us : Go thy ways to a nunnery. Where's your father?
Oph. At home, my lord.
Ham. Let the doors be shut upon him, that he
may play the fool nowhere but in's own house.
Farewell.
Oph. O, help him, you sweet heavens !
Ham. If thou dost marry, I'll give thee this
plague for thy dowry ; Be thou as chaste as ice,
as pure as snow, thou shalt not escape calumny.
Get thee to a nunnery ; farewell : Or, if thou
wilt needs marry, marry a fool ; for wise men
know well enough what monsters you make of
them. To a nunnery, go ; and quickly too.
Farewell.
Oph. Heavenly powers, restore him !
Ham. I have heard of your paintings too, well
enough ; Nature hath given you one face, and you
make yourselves another : you jig, you amble,
and you lisp, and nick-name God's creatures,
and make your wantonness your ignorance : Go
to ; I'll no more of 't ; it hath made me mad. I
say, we will have no more marriages : those that
are married already, all but one, shall live ; the
rest shall keep as they are. To a nunnery, go.
     [*Exit* HAM.
Oph. O, what a noble mind is here o'erthrown !
The courtier's, soldier's, scholar's, eye, tongue,
sword ;
The expectancy and rose of the fair state,
The glass of fashion, and the mould of form,
The observ'd of all observers! quite, quite down!
And I, of ladies most deject and wretched,
That suck'd the honey of his music vows,
Now see that noble and most sovereign reason,
Like sweet bells jangled, out of tune and harsh.;
That unmatch'd form and feature of blown youth,
Blasted with ecstasy : ‡‡ O, woe is me!
To have seen what I have seen, see what I see!

Re-enter KING *and* POLONIUS.

King. Love! his affections do not that way tend ;
Nor what he spake, though it lack'd form a little,
Was not like madness. There's something in his
O'er which his melancholy sits on brood ; [soul,
And, I do doubt, the hatch and the disclose
Will be some danger : Which for to prevent,
I have, in quick determination,   [land,
Thus set it down ; He shall with speed to Eng-
For the demand of our neglected tribute :
Haply, the seas, and countries different,
With variable objects, shall expel

FIG. 5. Format of former days. IV—In the edition of Thomas Bowdler, 1888.

piracies. In fact, he divides the quartos into the "bad" quartos published in "maimed or deformed" manner, and the "good" quartos whose texts were perfectly presentable; an argument which is given substance when it is realized that Heminge and Condell copied the text of the "good" quartos when printing the First Folio.

Derek Savage, in his *Hamlet and the Pirates*, makes the interesting suggestion that Shakespeare was in league with the pirates:

> It must be remembered that, having disposed of it to the company, Shakespeare no longer possessed rights over his manuscript, so that if (as I believe) he *had* wanted to publish it, he was powerless to do so except with their consent—and their consent could not be expected to be forthcoming for a play with such excellent prospects of long life in the theatre's repertory.

G. I. Duthie, of Aberdeen University has written *The "Bad" Quarto of Hamlet: a critical study*.

Perhaps the most exciting of all these bibliographical studies, however, is that edited by A. W. Pollard entitled *Shakespeare's Hand in the Play of Sir Thomas More*; papers by Alfred W. Pollard, W. W. Greg, E. Maunde Thompson, J. Dover Wilson, and R. W. Chambers, with the text of the *Ill May Day* scenes edited by W. W. Greg. Pollard writes:

> The object of this book is to strengthen the evidence of the existence (in the Harleian MS 7368 at the British Museum) of three pages written by Shakespeare in his own hand as part of the play of *Sir Thomas More*. The contributors have tried not to be over eager in pressing their contention, or to claim more than they can make good.

C. J. Sisson has performed a valuable task in his 2-volume study entitled *New Readings in Shakespeare*. Volume 1 deals with the comedies and poems, and volume 2 with the histories and tragedies. In the introduction, in volume 1, Sisson writes: "This book is an attempt to survey the principal proposals made during the lifetime of its readers for the restoration of the true text of Shakespeare". This introduction is a useful short account of the problems involved in restoring this text.

An authoritative summary of the textual problems is to be found in a volume of British Academy lectures, published under the title *Aspects of Shakespeare*, in which A. W. Pollard writes on 'Foundations of Shakespeare's Text'.

Modern editors have a very great respect for the punctuation of the Elizabethan printers, largely due to the work of Percy Simpson, whose book *Shakespearian Punctuation* was published in 1911 and whose conclusions have been generally accepted since, more especially since the attacks on the book which appeared after its publication were weightily condemned by Sir E. K. Chambers as "ill-conceived". Martin Seymour-Smith writes in his recent edition of the *Sonnets* that "Simpson performed an invaluable service in pointing out that the stopping in Shakespearian texts had been governed to a large extent by considerations of rhythm; he was mostly concerned with the Folio and his examples demonstrate convincingly the correctness of the original text".

At the end of the day, however, it was none of these men who published the most acceptable modern text of the complete plays, but Peter Alexander, who wrote on 'Restoring Shakespeare: the modern editor's task', in vol. 5 of *Shakespeare Survey*. This is what Dover Wilson has to say of his work:

> In 1951 an up-to-date scholarly edition of Shakespeare in one volume was published by Peter Alexander of Glasgow, the only complete text to appear in this country since Pollard wrote in 1909, except M. R. Ridley's "New Temple Shakespeare" which is an interesting attempt but too early to have availed itself of our present knowledge. In the light of that knowledge the text of *Richard III* was found to be so different from that printed in the old "Cambridge Shakespeare" or the "Globe" that Alexander actually departed from them in some 1500 readings . . . and in an edition of the play now in the press, I have ventured with the help of others by emendation to add over sixty more new readings.

So the "revolution" is still in progress and Dover Wilson writes:

> There can be no doubt that our current Shakespeares are a great deal nearer to what Shakespeare wrote than the original printed editions. Nevertheless, I repeat, we must begin re-editing them all over again, since despite everything editors . . . have effected in detail, they were wrong in principle.

The layman is inclined to throw up his hands in horror and exclaim "Great Heavens, are we never going to get it right, even after 400 years!" But if he really wants to know in some detail what the problems are, and is not satisfied with the works already quoted, let him read *Textual and Literary Criticism* by Fredson Bowers, especially the chapter 'New textual criticism of Shakespeare', or a paper by Fredson Bowers in vol. XX of *Studies in Bibliography* entitled 'To-day's Shakespeare texts and to-morrow's'.

Far be it from me to attempt to carry the story further; but I have left till the last the most enthralling account of the work of the bibliographers, namely Professor F. P. Wilson's 'Shakespeare and the new bibliography' which is printed in *The Bibliographical Society, 1892–1942: studies in retrospect*.

Scholars find the most acceptable edition of the complete works of Shakespeare that edited, with an introduction and glossary, by Peter Alexander. It is not a particularly handsome volume; the print is on the small side, and in my opinion Shakespeare's complete works cannot be comfortably contained in one volume. Even the great First to Fourth Folios are too massive for normal reading, and require to be spread out on a sturdy lectern. Professor Alexander, in this 1-volume edition, divided Shakespeare's career into four periods as follows:

  I Shakespeare's arrival in London, up to his joining the Lord Chamberlain's men.
 II Up to the opening of the Globe Theatre in 1599.
III Up to the taking over of the Blackfriars theatre, 1608.
IV Up to the burning of the Globe, 1613.

When the Globe disappeared gloriously in a holocaust of flame, during a too realistic performance of *Henry VIII*, no one was hurt save one man who, according to Sir Henry Wotton, was nearly "broiled in his breeches", but some scholars think some of Shakespeare's manuscripts may have perished in the flames. At any rate, the event is the effectual end of Shakespeare's career.

The most easily accessible of modern editions of the plays are those which appear in paperback. The first of these on the scene was the *Penguin Shakespeare*, originally edited by G. B. Harrison, with a clear, well-printed text, prepared previously to the appearance of the Alexander edition, with brief notes assembled at the end of the volume, and a glossary to help the multitude unfamiliar with Elizabethan English. Each volume begins with a short review of Shakespeare's career and the conditions of the Elizabethan theatre. This edition is being superseded by the *New Penguin Shakespeare*, whose general editor is T. J. B. Spencer, Professor of English Language and Literature and Director of the Shakespeare Institute, University of Birmingham. The first six plays to be published in this series are *Romeo and Juliet*, *Julius Caesar*, *Coriolanus*, *Midsummer Night's Dream*, *Macbeth*, and *The Merchant of Venice*. Each play is edited by a different authority who provides as an introduction a 20–30 page critical essay on the play. The text is not interrupted by any notes, these being gathered in a 'Commentary' at the back of each volume, extending to 150 or more pages. There is a brief account of the text with a summary of variant readings. In fact, this series is a beautiful marriage of the popular and the scholarly. The dashing cover illustrations by Pierre Clayette are, in my opinion, a notable addition to Shakespeare-inspired art.

The Signet edition is edited by Sylvan Barnet, who writes a general introduction. Each play is edited by a notable authority who provides notes on the text which are printed in small type at the foot of each page. After the play comes a brief survey of the history of the text, then a very useful anthology of critical pieces. The *Hamlet* for instance, has an anthology of essays by such critics as Coleridge, Bradley, Granville-Barker, and Maynard Mack. As in the *New Penguin Shakespeare*, there is a bibliography of suggested additional reading. These bibliographies are probably the most up to date at present available in print.

The *Cambridge Pocket Shakespeare*, published in hard covers, is the ideal text to take to the theatre with you. There are no notes to interrupt the text prepared by the editors of the *Cambridge Shakespeare*, Sir Arthur Quiller-Couch and John Dover Wilson, latterly assisted by J. C. Maxwell. A brief glossary is appended to each volume. Another good edition for the theatre, or the fireside when viewing a T.V. presentation, is the *Folger Library General Reader's Shakespeare*, edited by Louis B. Wright. The editor has printed his explanatory notes on the right-hand page throughout and the text on the left-hand page, so it is possible to read the text without referring to the notes (or vice versa), but if elucidation is required, the notes are ready to hand. Preliminary to the text there is a "brief statement of essential information about Shakespeare and his stage". The books have a squarish, sturdy format, and are available bound in cloth as well as in paperback.

Of modern hard-back editions, the two which are most in favour, and certainly the two most presentably printed, are *The New Shakespeare*, appearing now in dashing red jackets, and *The Arden Shakespeare*, an old favourite, now being re-edited in larger, brightly jacketed volumes, with notes, which take up in double column about half of every page. The general editors of the Arden series are Harold F. Brooks and Harold Jenkins. Each volume has its own particular editor responsible for a long and detailed introduction of up to 100 pages. The sources are uncovered, the subtleties argued, the stage history retailed, the themes discussed, and so on. These introductions, in my opinion, are best read after the play has been seen acted, not once, but several times; then with a good knowledge of the play and with the impact of the drama still in the mind, the reader can meet the learned arguments of the editor on something like equal terms. Of course, these can, with deepening knowledge, illuminate and refresh the reader's appreciation.

Next, two de luxe editions, bound in a manner that will grace the shelves of any private library, and printed to be easily read. First, *The London Shakespeare: a new annotated and critical edition of the Complete Works*, in 6 volumes, edited by the late John Munro, sometime assistant director of the Early English Text Society, with an introduction by G. W. G. Wickham, Head of the Department of Drama, University of Bristol. This edition has brief glossary notes at the foot of each page, with a short introduction to each play. The first volume has a fairly extensive bibliography of relevant works. Second, *The Complete Works of Shakespeare*, text and order of the First Folio with Quarto variants and a choice of modern readings noted marginally, edited by Herbert Farjeon. The editor wrote a short introduction but died before the completion of the edition, which was finished by Ivor Brown. There are no glossaries or notes. This is a scholar's edition, printed impeccably on delightful paper by the Nonesuch Press, in 6 volumes, the last containing the *Poems*.

A 1-volume edition, readable without strain and edited by C. J. Sisson, Professor of Modern English Literature in the University of London, is well-proportioned, bound sturdily but with elegance, the print big enough to be read easily, despite the double columns. The text is prefaced by a group of short essays on Shakespearean problems. There is an index of characters and a bibliography. A notable feature is the inclusion of the full text of the play *Sir Thomas More*. Another readable edition in 1 volume is *The Complete Works of Shakespeare* edited by George Lyman Kittredge, Professor of English Literature at Harvard. The plays follow the First Folio order and text except that *Two Noble Kinsmen* is included here. The lines are numbered to facilitate reference from Bartlett's *Concordance* and Schmidt's *Shakespeare–Lexicon*. The text is spelt and punctuated according to modern practice. There is a brief, 2-page introduction to each play, and at the end of the book a comprehensive glossary. The text is printed on strong, thin, opaque paper in double columns. The *Sonnets,* and all the poems, even *The Lover's Complaint*, are included.

In this chapter should be mentioned those standard reference books which are designed to make possible the identification of quotations, or a search for some desired extract or meaning, or piece of information concerning a detail in the plays or poems.

C. T. Onions' *A Shakespeare Glossary* is "an analysis of Shakespeare's vocabulary conducted in the light of the results published in the great Oxford English Dictionary." Its aim is to supply "definitions and illustrations of words or series of words now obsolete or surviving only in provincial or archaic use". Onions, of course, was one of the editors of the *Oxford English Dictionary*. A valuable handbook to linguistic examination of the works is A. C. Partridge's *Orthography in Shakespeare*. The author defines orthography as "that part of writing, peculiar to author, scribe,

Greg, W. W. A Descriptive Catalogue of the Early Editions of the Works of Shakespeare preserved in the Library of Eton College. Oxford, [1909].

Shaw, A. C. Birmingham Free Libraries: Index to the Shakespeare Memorial Library. 3 pts, Birmingham, 1900–3.

Scherzer, Jane. American Editions of Shakespeare, 1753–1866. PMLA. xxii, 1907.

Pollard, A. W. Shakespeare Folios and Quartos, 1594–1685. 1909.

Katalog der Bibliothek der Deutschen Shakespeare-Gesellschaft. Weimar, 1909.

Aldis, H. G., Moorman, F. W., Walder, Ernest and Robertson, J. G. Shakespeare. CHEL. vol. v, 1910.

A Catalogue of the Shakespeare Exhibition held in the Bodleian Library to commemorate the Death of Shakespeare. Oxford, 1916.

Bartlett, H. C. Catalogue of the Exhibition of Shakespeareana held at the New York Public Library in Commemoration of the Tercentenary of Shakespeare's Death. New York, 1917.

Herford, C. H. A Sketch of Recent Shakespearean Investigation, 1893–1923. 1923. [Critical survey.]

Gollancz, Sir Israel. In Commemoration of the First Folio Tercentenary. A Resetting of the Preliminary Matter of the First Folio, with a Catalogue of Shakespeareana exhibited in the Hall of the Company of Stationers. 1923.

Guide to the MSS. and Printed Books exhibited in Celebration of the Tercentenary of the First Folio. 1923. [BM. Ed. A. W. Pollard.]

Specimens of Shakespeareana in the Bodleian Library at Oxford. Oxford, 1927.

A Companion to Shakespeare Studies. Ed. H. Granville-Barker and G. B. Harrison, Cambridge, 1934. ['Reading List' with comments, pp. 347–68.]

Ford, H. L. Shakespeare, 1700–1740. A Collation of the Editions and Separate Plays. Lavorrick, 1935 (priv. ptd).

B. SHAKESPEARE SOCIETIES AND PERIODICALS

[See F. S. Boas, Shakespeare Societies, Past and Present, Shakespeare Rev. i, 1928.]

Shakespeare Society. 1841–52. [48 publications, 1841–53. For titles see *Jaggard*, pp. 606–7.]

Deutsche Shakespeare-Gesellschaft. 1864–. [Jahrbuch, Berlin, 1865–.]

New Shakspere Society. 1874–86. [27 publications. For titles and contents see *Jaggard*, pp. 228–31.]

New York Shakespeare Society. 1885–. [publications, New York, 1885–1903. 1 titles see *Jaggard*, p. 232.]

Shakespeare Association. 1917–. [18 pa phlets, Oxford, 1917–35. For titles *Ebisch and Schücking*, p. 171. Also publish texts, facsimiles and critical studies.]

Shakespeare Association of America. 192 [Annual Bulletin, New York, 1926–.]

Shakespeare Review. Stratford-on-Av 1928–.

II. THE LIFE AND PERSONALITY OF SHAKESPEARE

A. SHAKESPEARE'S LIFE

[*Ebisch and Schücking*, pp. 23–32; *Chambe* vol. i, chs. i–iii.]

(1) THE DOCUMENTS

[*Chambers*, vol. ii, Appendix A.]

Lambert, D. H. Cartae Shakespearean Shakespeare Documents. A Chronologic Catalogue of Extant Evidence. 1904.

Neilson, W. A. and Thorndike, A. H. T Facts about Shakespeare. New Yo 1913, 1931 (rev.).

Brooke, C. F. T. Shakespeare of Stratfor A Handbook for Students. New Have 1926.

Butler, Pierce. Materials for the Life Shakespeare. Chapel Hill, North Caroli 1932.

[The principal forgeries are listed *Chambers*, vol. ii, Appendix F. For t literature provoked by the forgeries of Irela and Collier, and the alleged forgeries Cunningham, see *Ebisch and Schücking*, 24–6, and the following:]

Stamp, A. E. The Disputed Rev Accounts. Shakespeare Ass. 1930.

Klein, D. The Case of Forman's 'Boc of Plaies.' PQ. xi, 1932.

Tannenbaum, S. A. More about t Forged Revels Accounts. New Yo 1932.

—— Shaksperian Scraps and Other E zabethan Fragments. New York, 19 [Various Collier forgeries.]

(2) THE PRINCIPAL BIOGRAPHIES

[The early biographical notes of Full Aubrey, etc. are listed below, p. 592.]

Rowe, Nicholas. Some Account of the Li &c. of Mr William Shakespear. [Prefix to his edn of The Works, 1709.]

Drake, Nathan. Shakespeare and his Tim 2 vols. 1817.

FIG. 6. The bibliographical apparatus. I—From *The Cambridge Bibliography of English Literature*, edited by F. W. Bateson, vol. 1 (with the permission of Cambridge University Press).

Raleigh, Sir Walter. 1942. SPROTT, S. E. Ralegh's 'Sceptic' and the Elizabethan Translation of Sextus Empiricus. PQ., Apr., XLII, 166–75.

Sackville, Thomas. 1943. HOWARTH, R. G. Thomas Sackville and a Mirror for Magistrates. ESA., Mar., VI, 77–99.

Sandys, Sir Edwin. 1944. RABB, THEODORE K. The Editions of Sir Edwin Sandys's 'Relation of the State of Religion'. HLQ., Aug., XXVI, 323–36.

Selimus. 1945. JACQUOT, JEAN. A propos du 'Tragicall Raigne of Selimus': Le problème des emprunts aux classiques à la Renaissance. EA., Oct., XVI, 345–50.

Shakespeare, William

EDITIONS

1946. ARGUILE, H. and K. R. NICOL (eds.). King Henry V. Cape Town: Maskew Miller. pp. 174.

1947. CAIRNCROSS, ANDREW S. (ed.). The First Part of King Henry VI. (Bibl. 1962, 2525.) Rev. by George Walton Williams in ELN., I, 62–5; by Cyrus Hoy in SQ., XIV, 466–7.

1948. DUTHIE, G. I. and J. DOVER WILSON (eds.). King Lear. (Bibl. 1960, 2098.) Rev. by Nicholas Brooke in DUJ., XXIV, 147–50.

1949. FOAKES, R. A. (ed.). The Comedy of Errors. (Bibl. 1962, 2527.) Rev. by George Walton Williams in ELN., I, 62–5; by J. H. P. Pafford in DUJ., XXIV, 150–2.

1950. FURNESS, H. H. (ed.). A New Variorum Edition of Shakespeare. Reissue of six vols.: Hamlet (2 vols.); King Lear; Macbeth; Othello; Romeo and Juliet. N.Y.: Dover; London: Constable. pp. 473, 429; 503; 566; 471; 480.

1951. HOENIGER, F. D. (ed.). Pericles. London: Methuen; Cambridge, Mass.: Harvard Univ. Press. pp. 188. (Arden Shakespeare.) Rev. by M. Mincoff in E. Studies, XLIV, 459–60.

1952. HOY, CYRUS (ed.). Hamlet: An Authoritative Text, Intellectual Background, Extracts from the Sources, Essays in Criticism. N.Y.: Norton. (Norton Critical Ed.)

1953. HUGO, FRANCOIS-VICTOR (trans.). Théâtre complet de Shakespeare. Ed. by J. B. FORT. 2 vols. Paris: Garnier, 1961. pp. 1046; 1222. Rev. by Milton Crane in SQ., XIV, 468–9; by Curt A. Zimansky in SQ., XIV, 173–4.

1954. HUMPHREYS, A. R. (ed.). The First Part of King Henry IV. (Bibl. 1960, 2103.) Rev. by Mary Lascelles in MLR., LVIII, 237.

1955. MAXWELL, J. C. (ed.). King Henry VIII. (Bibl. 1962, 2533.) Rev. by J. H. P. Pafford in DUJ., XXIV, 150–2; by E. A. J. Honigmann in RES., XIV, 404–7.

1956. MUNNIK, P. DE (ed.). The Tempest. Johannesburg: Voortrekkerpers. pp. 108.

1957. —— Julius Caesar. Johannesburg: Voortrekkerpers. pp. 132.

FIG. 7. The bibliographical apparatus. II—From *Annual Bibliography of English Language and Literature, 1963* (with the permission of the editor, Miss M. Rigby).

Shakespeare
See also DRAMA, *Great Britain.*

Bibliography

BAILEY (Sir WILLIAM HENRY)
—— The " 'Bradshaw' " of Shakespeare. In praise of the new catalogue of the Birmingham Shakespeare Memorial Library. pp. 14. *Cornish Bros.: Birmingham; Sherratt & Hughes: Manchester,* [1904 ?] 8°. 011919. cc. 4.

BETHLEHEM, *Pennsylvania.—Lehigh University.—Lucy Packer Linderman Memorial Library.*
—— The Shakespeare Folios and the Forgeries of Shakespeare's Handwriting in the Lucy Packer Linderman Memorial Library of Lehigh University, with a list of original folios in American libraries. By Robert Metcalf Smith . . . with the assistance of Howard Seavoy Leach. [With illustrations.] pp. 47. *Bethlehem,* 1927. 8°. [*Lehigh University. Institute of Research. Circular no. 7.*] · Ac. 2692. qd.

FISHER (SIDNEY)
—— An Exhibit of Shakespeare Books, from the Collection of Mr. Sidney Fisher of Montreal, *etc.* [With illustrations.] pp. 38. *Halcyon Press: Montreal,* 1956. 8°. 11928. e. 11.

HAHN (WIKTOR)
—— Shakespeare w Polsce. Bibliografia. pp. xix. 386. *Wrocław,* 1958. 8°. 2785. cm. 1.

STRATFORD-UPON-AVON.—*Shakespeare Memorial Library.*
—— Items of Interest to Theatre Research Workers. ff. 4. [*Stratford-upon-Avon,*] 1957. fol. 011768. d. 6.

SCHROEDER (JOHN W.)
—— The Great Folio of 1623. Shakespeare's plays in the printing house. pp. xi. 125. pl. 29. *Shoe String Press: [Hamden,]* 1956. 8°. 011768. p. 9.

EATON (SEYMOUR)
—— Shakespeare Rare Print Collection. Edited by S. Eaton. 12 pt. *R. G. Kennedy & Co.: Philadelphia,* 1900. 4°. Cup. 500. cc. 7.

Biography
See also below, Authorship Controversy.

BROWN (IVOR JOHN CARNEGIE)
—— Shakespeare. Specially revised and abridged by the author. pp. 254. *Collins: London,* 1957. 8°. [*Comet Books. no. 6.*] W.P. 6891/6.

—— William Shakespeare. Illustrated by Robert Hodgson. pp. 84. *Thomas Nelson & Sons: Edinburgh,* [1958.] 8°. 11768. f. 16.

DAWSON (GILES EDWIN)
—— The Life of William Shakespeare. [With illustrations, including a portrait.] pp. 34. *Folger Shakespeare Library: Washington,* 1958. 8°. [*Folger Booklets on Tudor and Stuart Civilisation.*] W.P. 16254/6.

FOX (LEVI)
—— William Shakespeare. A concise life. [With illustrations, including portraits.] *Jarrold & Sons: Norwich,* [1959.] 16°. 011768. ff. 5.

HALLIDAY (FRANK ERNEST)
—— Shakespeare. A pictorial biography. pp. 147. *Thames & Hudson: London,* 1956. 8°. 011768. g. 9.

PINETON (CLARA LONGWORTH DE) *Countess de Chambrun.*
—— [Shakespeare retrouvé.] Shakespeare: a portrait restored. [Translated by the author.] pp. ix. 406. *Hollis & Carter: London,* 1957. 8°. 011768. g. 14.

BLUMENTHAL (WALTER HART)
—— The Mermaid Myth. Shakespeare not among those present. pp. 32. *Westholm Publications: Hanover, N. H.,* 1959. 8°. 011768. p. 6.

MARTIN (WILLIAM) *M.A., LL.D., F.S.A.*
—— Shakespeare and Bankside. A perambulation from the Church of S. Saviour's, Southwark, *etc.* [With illustrations.] pp. 12. [1904.] 4°. 011768. l. 1.

Criticism

APOLLONIO (MARIO)
—— Shakespeare. pp. 204. *Brescia,* 1941. 8°. 011768. df. 26.

BARKER (HARLEY GRANVILLE)
—— Prefaces to Shakespeare. 2 vol. *B. T. Batsford: London,* 1958, 8°. 011768. l. 2.

BENEDEK (MARCELL)
—— Shakespeare. (A függelékek készítette és az illusztrá- ciókat összeállította Staud Géza.) [With plates, including a portrait.] pp. 415. *Budapest,* 1957. 8°. 011768. k. 3.

BIANCOTTI (ANGIOLO)
—— Guglielmo Shakespeare. [With plates, including a por- trait.] pp. vi. 303. *Torino,* 1957. 8°. 11768. bb, 44.

BRUNNER (CARL) *of Vienna.*
—— William Shakespeare. [With plates, including a por- trait.] pp. viii. 232. *Tübingen,* 1957. 8°. 011768. h. 3.

BURTON (HARRY MCGUIRE)
—— Shakespeare and his Plays . . . With illustrations . . . by Richard G. Robinson. pp. 68. *Methuen & Co.: London,* 1958. 8°. [*Methuen's Outlines.*] W.P. a. 543/36.

CRAIG (HARDIN)
—— An Interpretation of Shakespeare. pp. ix. 400. *Citadel Press: New York,* 1949. 8°. 011768. g. 6.

ELLING (CHRISTIAN)
—— Shakespeare. Indsyn i hans verden og dens poesi. [With plates.] *København,* 1959– . fol. 011768. d. 7.

GARRETT (JOHN WALTER PERCY)
—— More Talking of Shakespeare. Edited by J. Garrett. pp. ix. 190. *Longmans: London,* 1959. 8°. 011768. p. 1.

HALLIDAY (FRANK ERNEST)
—— Shakespeare in his Age. [With plates.] pp. xvi. 362. *Gerald Duckworth & Co.: London,* 1956. 8°. 011768. ee. 15.

HARRISON (GEORGE BAGSHAWE)
—— Introducing Shakespeare. (Revised edition, reprinted.) pp. 174. *Penguin Books: Harmondsworth,* 1957. 8°. [*Pelican Books. no. A43.*] 012209. d. 4/43.

HERGEŠIĆ (IVO)
—— Shakespeare, Molière, Goethe. Književno-kazališne studije, pp. 299, pl. viii. *Zagreb,* 1957 [1958]. 8°. 011768. eee. 24.

HOWARTH (ROBERT GUY)
—— Shakespeare by Air. Broadcasts to schools. pp. 64. *Angus & Robertson: Sydney,* 1957. 8°. 011768. de. 9.

ILLSLEY (WILLIAM ALLEN)
—— A Shakespeare Manual for Schools. [With illustrations.] pp. 95. *University Press: Cambridge,* 1957. 8°. 011768. eee. 5.

LUETHI (MAX)
—— Shakespeares Dramen. pp. 473. *Berlin,* 1957. 8°. 011768. c. 18.

MOROZOV (MIKHAIL MIKHAILOVICH)
—— Шекспир . . . 2-е издание. pp. 213, *Москва,* 1956. 8°. 11768. b. 39.

MACINTOSH (JOAN)
—— An Introduction to Shakespeare. pp. 144. *Macmillan & Co.: London,* 1957. 8°. 011768. eee. 7.

PARIS (JEAN) *Assistant in French at the University of Aber- deen.*
—— Connaissance de Shakespeare. Présentations et tra- ductions de Jean Paris. pp. 126. *Paris,* 1956. 8°. [*Cahiers de la Compagnie Madeleine Renaud Jean-Louis Barrault. année 4. cahier 16.*] W.P.1447/16.

PARRY (JOHN) *M.A.*
—— A Guide to Shakespeare. pp. 71. *George G. Harrap & Co.: London,* 1958. 8°. [*Harrap's African Guide Series.*] W.P. 16363/1.

—— A Guide to Shakespeare for Malayan Students. pp. 71. *George G. Harrap & Co.: London,* 1956. 8°. 011768. de. 41.

RIDLEY (MAURICE ROY)
—— Shakespeare's Plays. A commentary. pp. vi. 227. *J. M. Dent & Sons: London,* 1957. 8°. 011768. bb. 43.

REBORA (PIERO)
—— Shakespeare. La vita, l'opera, il messaggio. pp. 347. [*Milan,*] 1958. 8°. 011768. a. 48.

SHAKESPEARE (WILLIAM) [*Selections and Extracts.— French.*]
—— Shakespeare par lui même. Images et textes présentés par Jean Paris. [With illustrations.] pp. 191. *Paris,* 1954. 8°. 011768. a. 39.

TRAVERS (DEREK ANTONA)
—— An Approach to Shakespeare . . . Second edition, revised & enlarged. pp. 304. *Sands & Co.: [London] & Glasgow,* [1957.] 8° 11689. ff. 13.

WEBSTER (MARGARET)
—— Shakespeare today, *etc.* pp. 318. *J. M. Dent & Sons: London,* 1957. 8°. 011768. ee.

HALER (ALBERT)
—— Iz tudih knjizevnosti. [Including essays on some Shakespeare's plays.] pp. 215. *Zagreb,* 1941. 8°. 011768. a.

SHAKESPEARE (WILLIAM) [*Appendix.—Criticism.*]
—— Shakespeare. A review and a preview. [Articles various authors. With plates.] pp. 25. *Limited Editions Club: New York,* [1939.] fol. C. 105. e.

SJÖGREN (GUNNAR)
—— Var Othello neger, och andra Shakespeareproblem. [With plates.] pp. 196. *Stockholm,* 1958. 8°. 011768. eee.

RUSSIA.—*Всероссийское Театральное Общество.*
—— Шекспировский сборник. [With summaries in English.] 1958, *etc. Москва,* [1959– .] 8°. 011768. h.

SHAKESPEARE FELLOWSHIP
—— The Shakespeare Fellowship News-Letter. Sept. 195 *etc.* [*London.*] 1954– . 8°. P.P. 5985. fb

BERTON (JEAN CLAUDE)
—— Shakespeare et Claudel. Le temps et l'espace au théâ. pp. 224. *Genève, Paris; Millan* [printed], 1958. 8°. 11871. tt.

EHRL (CHARLOTTE)
—— Sprachstil und Charakter bei Shakespeare. pp. 195 *Heidelberg,* 1957. 8°. [*Schriftenreihe der Deutschen Shakespeare-Gesellschaft. Neue Folge. Bd. 6.*] Ac. 9425

EVANS (Sir BENJAMIN IFOR)
—— The Language of Shakespeare's Plays. (Second edition.) pp. xi. 216. *Methuen & Co.: London,* 1959. 8°. 011768. f.

GERSTNER-HIRZEL (ARTHUR)
—— The Economy of Action and Word in Shakespeare Plays. Inaugural-Dissertation, *etc.* pp. 135. *Gassman Solothurn,* 1957. 8°. 011768. p.

HEUSER (GEORG)
—— Die aktlose Dramaturgie William Shakespeares. Ein Untersuchung über das Problem der Akteinteilung un angeblichen Aktstruktur der Shakespeareschen Dramen Inauguraldissertation, *etc.* pp. 430. *Marburg,* 1956. 8°. Ac. 9425

MAHOOD (M. M.)
—— Shakespeare's Wordplay. pp. 192. *Methuen & Co. London,* 1957. 8°. 011768. ee. 22

PRICE (HEREWARD THIMBLEBY)
—— Construction in Shakespeare. pp. 42. [*Ann Arbo 1951. 8°. [University of Michigan Contributions Modern Philology. no. 17.*] Ac. 2685/9

SCHLUETER (KURT)
—— Shakespeares dramatische Erzählkunst. pp. 159. *Heidelberg,* 1958. 8°. [*Schriftenreihe der Deutschen Shakespeare-Gesellschaft. Neue Folge. Bd. 7.*] Ac. 9425

SHACKFORD (MARTHA HALE)
—— Shakespeare, Sophocles: dramatic modes. pp. 2. *Suburban Press: Natick,* [1957.] 8°. 011768. ee. 20

SNUGGS (HENRY LAWRENCE)
—— Shakespeare and Five Acts. Studies in a dramatic convention. pp. 144. *Vantage Press: New Yor* [1960.] 8°. 011768. eee. 2.

TSCHOPP (ELISABETH)
—— Zur Verteilung von Vers und Prosa in Shakespear Dramen. pp. vii. 118. *Bern,* 1956. 8°. [*Schweizer anglistische Arbeiten. Bd. 41.*] W.P. 1693/4.

BRADLEY (ANDREW CECIL)
—— Shakespearean Tragedy, *etc.* pp. xv. 432. *Macmillan Co.: London,* 1957. 8°. [*St. Martin's Library.*] W.P. 4443/7

SIEGEL (PAUL N.)
—— Shakespearean Tragedy and the Elizabethan Compromise. pp. xvi. 243. *New York University Press New York,* 1957. 8°. 011761. f. 4.

STIRLING (BRENTS)
—— Unity in Shakespearian Tragedy. The interplay of them and character. pp. viii. 212. *Columbia University Press New York,* 1956. 8°. 011768. ee. 16

FIG. 8. The bibliographical apparatus. III—From the British Museum's *Subject Index of Books Acquired, 1956–60* (with the permission of the Trustees of the British Museum).

SHAKESPEARE, William
Exposition, Criticism, Soliloquies
CLEMEN, Wolfgang
Shakespeare's soliloquies : the Presidential
Address of the Modern Humanities Research Assoc-
iation, 1964. London, Cambridge U.P., 3/6. Apr
[1964]. [1],27p. 18½cm. Sd. (Modern Humani-
ties Research Association. Presidential
addresses—1964)
(B64-8927)

Characters. Pathological psychology
SCOTT, William Inglis Dunn
Shakespeare's melancholics; with a foreword by Henry
Yellowlees. London, Mills & Boon, 21/-. Dec 1962.
192p. table, bibliog. 22½cm.
'...eight Shakespearean characters—Antonio the Merchant of
Venice, Don John, Orsino, Jaques, Hamlet, Timon, Pericles,
Leontes—who have in common the fact that Elizabethan
thought would have classed them all as 'melancholic,'
examined in the light of modern psychological knowledge.'—
wrapper.
(B63-406)

Characters. Comic characters
PALMER, John [Leslie]
Political and comic characters of Shakespeare. See
822.3—Shakespeare, William. Characters. Political
characters.

PRIESTLEY, John Boynton
The English comic characters. See 823.6/8—English
fiction, 1745-1849. Characters. Comic characters.

Characters. Political characters
PALMER, John [Leslie]
Political and comic characters of Shakespeare, by John
Palmer. London, Macmillan; New York, St. Martin's P.,
21/-. Sep 1961. [498]p. 21½cm. Sd. (Papermacs—
no.4)
2 vols. in 1. Various paging. Vol.1 originally published 1945;
vol.2 originally published 1946.
Subsidiary subject: 822.3 Shakespeare, William. Characters.
Comic characters.
(B61-10099)
Political and comic characters of Shakespeare. London,
Macmillan; New York, St. Martin's P., 35/-. Jun 1962.
xii,483p. 22½cm.
Originally published as two books: Political characters of
Shakespeare, 1945, and Comic characters of Shakespeare,
1946.
Subsidiary subject: 822.3—Shakespeare, William. Characters.
Comic characters.
(B62-10554)

Characters. Falstaff, Sir John
KAISER, Walter [Jacob]
Praisers of folly : Erasmus, Rabelais, Shakes-
peare. See 847.3—French humorous & satirical
prose. Rabelais, Francois. Gargantua and
Pantagruel. Characters. Panurge.

Exposition, Criticism. Authorship
GIBSON, Harry Norman
The Shakespeare claimants : a critical survey of four
of the principal theories concerning the authorship of
the Shakespearean plays. London, Methuen, 30/-. Jun
1962. 320p. 4plates(ports.), facsim., bibliog. 22½cm.
(B62-8536)
MUIR, Kenneth [Arthur]
Shakespeare as collaborator. London, Methuen, 16/-.
Jul 1960. xi,164p. 19cm.
(B60-11063)

Exposition, Criticism. Baconian theory
BACON, Delia [Salter]
—Exposition
HOPKINS, Vivian Constance
Prodigal Puritan. See 928.183—Biography. Bacon,
Delia [Salter].

JOHNSON, Edward Dudley [Hume]
Francis Bacon's maze : being a demonstration of the
sixth line word cipher in the first folio of the "Shake-
speare" plays. Canonbury Tower, London, N.1, Francis
Bacon Society, 12/-. 1960. vii,68p. tables. 28cm.
Sd. (Francis Bacon Society. Publications)
(B61-9520)

Exposition, Criticism. Burton theory
BROWNLEE, Alexander
William Shakespeare and Robert Burton. [Old Burgh-
clere, Newbury (Berks.), R. L. Cook], 27/6. [dMay
1960]. xi,337p. 22cm.
(B60-8427)

SHAKESPEARE, William
—Exposition, Criticism. De Vere theory
LE RICHE, Kathleen
Shakespeare in Essex. 36 Gloucester Walk, London,
W.8, K. Le Riche, 1/6. [dMar 1961]. 8p. 21½cm. Sd.
Reprinted from the Essex Review. Vol.61, Oct 1952.
(B61-6385)

—Exposition, Criticism. Elizabeth I theory
SWEET, George Elliott
Shake-speare, the mystery. London, Spearman,
21/-. Sep 1963. 200p. front.(port.), tables,
bibliog. 22½cm.
(B63-13823)

—Exposition, Criticism. Stanley theory
TITHERLEY, Arthur Walsh
Shakespeare: new side lights (overt and covert). Win-
chester, Warren, 30/-. [dAug]1961. viii,131p. 5plates
(incl. 4col.). 22cm.
(B61-15456)

—Special themes. Honour
WATSON, Curtis Brown
Shakespeare and the Renaissance concept of honor.
Princeton (N.J.), Princeton U.P.; [London, Oxford
U.P.], 60/-. 1960. xviii,471p. bibliog. 24½cm.
(B61-10006)

—Special themes. Love
HOLBROOK, David
The quest for love. See 823.91—English fiction.
Lawrence, David Herbert. Special themes. Love.

—Special themes. Religion
FRYE, Roland Mushat
Shakespeare and Christian doctrine. Princeton
(N.J.), Princeton U.P.; London, Oxford U.P., 35/-.
1963. ix,314p. bibliog. 22½cm.
(B64-8928)
MENDL, Robert William Sigismund
Revelation in Shakespeare : a study of the super-
natural, religious and spiritual elements in his
art. London, Calder, 35/-. Dec 1964. 223p.
bibliog. 21cm.
(B64-23486)

—Special subjects. Politics
BLOOM, Allan, and JAFFA, Harry Victor
Shakespeare's politics, by Allan Bloom with
Harry V. Jaffa. New York, London, Basic Books,
25/-. Sep [1964]. [9],150p. 22cm.
A study of 'The Merchant of Venice', 'Othello', Julius
Caesar' and 'King Lear'.
(B64-20799)

—Special subjects. Sea voyages
FALCONER, Alexander Frederick
Shakespeare and the sea, by Lieutenant-Commander
Alexander Frederick Falconer. London, Constable,
35/-. May 1964. xvi,164p. front. 22½cm.
(B64-11030)

—Collected works
Comedies—Exposition, Criticism
BROWN, John Russell
Shakespeare and his comedies. 2nd ed. with a new
chapter on the last comedies. London, Methuen, 21/-.
Oct 1962. 253p. 22½cm.
Previous ed. (B57-14119) 1957.
(B62-14446)

EVANS, Bertrand
Shakespeare's comedies. Oxford, Clarendon P., 42/-.
Sep 1960. xiii,337p. 22cm.
(B60-15407)

HUNTER, G   K
The late comedies [of] William Shakespeare. London,
published for the British Council and the National
Book League by Longmans, 2/6. Feb 1962. 63p.
4plates(facsims, bibliog. 22cm. Sd. ('British Book
News.' Bibliographical series of supplements, edited
by Bonamy Dobrée)
Contents: A midsummer-night's dream.—Much ado about
nothing.—As you like it.—Twelth night.
(B62-4360)

TRAVERSI, Derek Antona
William Shakespeare: the early comedies. London,
Longmans, Green, for the British Council and National
Book League, 2/6. May 1960. 46p. 4plates(facsims),
bibliog. 21½cm. Sd. ('British Book News.' Biblio-
graphical series of supplements—no.129)
Contents: The comedy of errors.—The taming of the shrew.—
Two gentlemen of Verona.—Love's labour's lost.
(B61-1193)

SHAKESPEARE, William
—Collected works
Comedies—Exposition, Criticism
TRAVERSI, Derek Antona
William Shakespeare : the early comedies, by
Derek Traversi. Revised ed. London, published
for the British Council and the National Book
League by Longmans, 2/6. Jun 1964. 60p.
4plates(facsims.), bibliog. Sd. ('British Book
News'. Bibliographical series of supplements,
edited by Bonamy Dobrée—no.129)
Contents: The comedy of errors.—Love's labour's
lost.—The merchant of Venice. Previous ed. (B61-1193)
1960.
(B64-16059)
WILSON, John Dover
Shakespeare's happy comedies. London, Faber, 25/-.
Nov 1962. 3-224p. 22½cm.
(B62-16848)

Histories—Exposition, Criticism
CAMPBELL, Lily Bess
Shakespeare's "Histories": mirrors of Eliza-
bethan policy. London, Methuen, 21/-. Jul
1964. [9],346p. 21½cm.
Originally published, San Marino (Cal.), Huntington
Library, 1947.
(B64-14623)

KNIGHTS, L   C
William Shakespeare : the histories. London,
published for the British Council and National Book
League by Longmans, 2/6. Oct 1962. 55p. 4plates,
bibliog. 21½cm. Sd. (British Book News.'
Bibliographical series of supplements on writers and
their work, edited by Bonamy Dobrée—no.151)
Contents: Richard III.—King John.—Richard II.—Henry V.
(B63-173)
LEECH, Clifford
Shakespeare : the Chronicles; Henry VI, Henry IV,
the merry wives of Windsor, Henry VIII. London,
published for the British Council and the National
Book League by Longmans, 2/6. May 1962. 47p.
front.(map), plates, bibliog. 21½cm. Sd. ('British
Book News.' Bibliographical series of supplements,
edited by Bonamy Dobrée—no.146)
(B62-9823)

REESE, Max Meredith
The cease of majesty : a study of Shakespeare's
history plays. London, Edward Arnold, 35/-. Oct
1961. ix,350p. 22½cm.
(B61-19100)
SEN GUPTA, Subodh Chandra
Shakespeare's historical plays. Oxford, Ox-
ford U.P., 25/-. [dNov] 1964. [9],172p.
22½cm.
(B64-22892)
SPRAGUE, Arthur Colby
Shakespeare's histories : plays for the stage.
103 Ralph Crt., London, W.2, Society for
Theatre Research, 30/-. Apr 1964. xii,167p.
front.(port.). 22½cm. (Society for Theatre
Research. Publications)
(B64-9875)
TILLYARD, Eustace Mandeville Wetenhall
Shakespeare's history plays. Harmondsworth,
Penguin, 8/6. Jun 1962. viii,336p. 20cm. Sd.
(Peregrine books—no.Y4)
Originally published, London, Chatto & Windus, 1944.
(B62-768)

Tragedies—Exposition, Criticism
CAMPBELL, Lily Bess
Shakespeare's tragic heroes : slaves of passion.
[New ed.]. London, Methuen, 21/-(14/- Sd.). May
1962. xii,296p. 13plates(facsims.). 20½cm.
Originally published, London, Cambridge U.P., 1930.
(B62-8203)
HARRISON, George Bagshawe
Shakespeare's tragedies. London, Routledge & K.
Paul, 8/6. Jun 1961. 277p. 22cm. Sd.
Originally published (B51-13076) 1951.
(B61-9521)
HOLLOWAY, [Christopher] John
The story of the night : studies in Shakespeare's
major tragedies. London, Routledge & K. Paul, 21/-.
Nov 1961. x,187p. 22½cm.
(B61-21034)
LAWLOR, John
The tragic sense in Shakespeare. London, Chatto &
Windus, 18/-. Sep 1960. 186p. 22½cm.

FIG. 9. The bibliographical apparatus. IV—From the British National
Bibliography *Cumulated Subject Catalogue*, 1955–59 (with the permission
of the Council of the B.N.B.).

B1703 Emerson, Elizabeth. *English Dramatic Critics of the Nineties and the Acting of the* "*New Theatre.*" DD, Bryn Mawr College, 1953.

B1704 Kemp, T. C. "Acting Shakespeare: Modern Tendencies in Playing and Production with Special Reference to Some Recent Productions." *ShS*, VII (1954), 121-127.

B1705 Leclerc, Hélène. "Scénographie et Architecture Théâtrale en Angleterre (Exposition à Londres, Juillet, 1955)." *RHT*, VIII (1956), 24-39.

B1706 Coghill, Nevill. "University Contributions to Shakespeare Production in England." *SJ*, 93 (1957), 175-185.

B1707 Walker, Roy. "Short of Shakespeare." *Listener*, May 2, 1957, pp. 728-729.

B1708 *Shakespeare im Britischen Theater. Eine vom British Council Zusammengestellte Ausstellung (Katalog).* Vienna: Theater in d. Josefsstadt, 1958. Pp. 16.

(b) AMERICA

B1709 Manser, Ruth B. *The Influence of the American Actress on the Development of the American Theatre from 1835 to 1935.* DD, New York University, 1938.

B1710 Wilson, Garff Bell. *American Styles and Theories of Acting from Edwin Forrest to David Belasco.* DD, Cornell University, 1940. Abstr. publ. in Cornell Univ. *Abstracts of Theses, 1940*, Ithaca, 1941.

B1711 Belcher, Fannin S., Jr. *The Place of the Negro in the Evolution of the American Theatre, 1767-1940.* DD, Yale University, 1946.

B1712 Schoell, Edwin R. *A Quantitative Analysis of the Contributions of the Community Theatre to the Development of the Drama.* DD, University of Denver, 1952.

B1713 West, L. Edna. *Contemporary Broadway Criticism.* DD, University of Wisconsin, 1952. Abstr. publ. in Univ. of Wisconsin *Summaries of Doctoral Dissertations, 1951/52*, Madison, 1953, pp. 404-405.

B1714 Downer, Alan S. "Shakespeare in the Contemporary American Theater." *SJ*, 93 (1957), 154-169.

B1715 Cox, Charles Wright. *The Evolution of the Stage Director in America.* DD, Northwestern University, 1958. Pp. 466. Mic 58-4764. *DA*, XVIII (1958), 1144. Publ. No. 24,900.

b. DRAMATURGIC PRINCIPLES OF SHAKESPEAREAN PRODUCTION (163;55)
(1) MAJOR DISCUSSIONS

B1716 Buzzini, Bertram G. "If Shakespeare Knew." *San Francisco Quart.*, II (1935), 21-24.

B1717 Brandl, A. "Eine neue Art, Shakespeare zu Spielen." Brandl, *Forschungen und Charakteristiken*, No. 184 (Berlin, 1936), 138-146. [Reprinted from *Deutsche Rundschau*, 123 (1905), 122 ff.]

B1718 Knight, G. Wilson. *Principles of Shakespearian Production.* London: Faber and Faber; New York: Macmillan, 1936. Pp. 246. Harmondsworth: Penguin Books, 1949. Pp. 224.
   Rev: *TLS*, May 2, 1936, p. 373; by W. J. Lawrence, *Spectator*, May 8, p. 848; by E. Martin Browne, *Criterion*, LXII, 143-146; by Frederick Laws, *NstN*, NS, XI, 897-898; *London Mercury*, XXXIV, 378; by T. R. Barnes, *Scrutiny*, V, 328-329; by Rosamond Gilder, *TAr*, XXI (1937), 330-331; by Mark Van Doren, *Nation* (N. Y.), 144 (1937), 188-189; by Everett M. Schreck, *QJS*, XXIII, 504-505; by William Empson, *Life and Letters Today*, XV, No. 5, 202; by H. Voaden, *Canadian Forum*, XVI, No. 191, 34.

B1719 Centeno, Augusto, ed. *The Intent of the Artist.* Princeton Univ. Press, 1941. Pp. 162.

B1720 Gassner, J. *Producing the Play.* New York, 1941. Pp. xxx, 744.
   Shak., pp. 450-460.

B1721 Mitchell, Lee. "The Effect of Modern Stage Conventions on Shakespeare." *TAr*, XXVI (1942), 447-451.

B1722 McLeod, A. *The Nature of the Relations Between the Theatre Audience, the Drama and the Mise-en-scène.* Abstr. in Cornell Univ. *Abstracts of Theses* (Ithaca), 1943, pp. 65-68.

B1723 Brook, P. "Style in Shakespearean Production." *Orpheus* (London), 1948, pp. 139-146.

B1724 MacLiammóir, M. "Three Shakespearean Productions: A Conversation." *ShS*, I (1948), 89-97.

B1725 Kutscher, Arthur. *Grundriss der Theaterwissenschaft.* Munich: Desch, 1949. Pp. 495.

B1726 Reynolds, G. F. "Shakespeare and His World: Staging Elizabethan Plays." *Listener*, XLII (Aug. 11, 1949), 223-224.

B1727 Bellman, Willard F. *An Approach to an Aesthetics of the Visual Production of the Drama.* DD, Northwestern University, 1950. Abstr. publ. by Northwestern Univ. in *Summaries of Doctoral Dissertations*, XVII (1950), Chicago and Evanston, pp. 86-89.

B1728 Byrne, Muriel St. Clare. "A Stratford Production: *Henry VIII.*" *ShS*, III (1950), 120-129.

B1729 Purdom, Charles Benjamin. *Producing Shakespeare.* London: Pitman, 1950; New York: British Book Centre, 1951. Pp. xii, 220.
   Rev: *TLS*, Jan. 12, 1951, p. 22; by Michael MacOwan, *Spectator*, Feb. 2, pp. 156, 158; by

FIG. 10. The bibliographical apparatus. V—From *A Classified Shakespeare Bibliography, 1936-1958*, by Gordon Ross Smith (copyright 1963, by the Pennsylvania State University; used with the permission of the Pennsylvania State University Press).

editor or printing-house, which is concerned with accidentals such as spelling, punctuation, elision, syncope and contractions generally". Still an invaluable source of information is Bartlett's famous *Concordance to the Plays of Shakespeare*, which also has a concordance to the poems. The line references are to the old Globe 1-volume edition of the works, and to facilitate references many more recent editions of the complete works are careful to keep to the same line numbering scheme. The concordance is arranged by keywords, under each of which quotations are arranged in groups, one play at a time. Even more massive than Bartlett is Burton Stevenson's *Book of Shakespeare Quotations*, which the author describes as being also a concordance and a glossary of the unique words and phrases in the plays and poems. The first 1759 pages give the quotations arranged by keywords, and there then follows an index to all these quotations. A handier volume, though necessarily selective, is D. C. Browning's *Everyman's Dictionary of Shakespeare Quotations*, which arranges the quotations under the headings of the titles of the plays, with the quotations in the order in which they appear in the play, reference to a desired phrase being made possible by an index of keywords. Alexander Schmidt's *Shakespeare–Lexicon* is sub-titled "a complete dictionary of all English words, phrases and constructions in the works of the poet", and when the author says "all" he means "all". Shakespeare's vocabulary was phenomenally extensive, and some enterprising researchers have declared that he used a greater proportion of the possible words than any other writer before or since. Indeed, over 7000 of the words he used only once. An enormous number of his phrases have passed into common use in the English language, such as "pitched battle", "unconsidered trifles", and so on.

The most comprehensive single-volume reference work for historical, biographical, and literary information is Oscar James Campbell's *A Shakespeare Encyclopaedia*, whose associate editor is Edward G. Quinn. This book carries under the entry for each play a very useful digest of information concerning the textual problems, sources, stage history, comment (by O. J. Campbell), and a small anthology of excerpts from typical critical writings from Johnson to the present day.

F. E. Halliday's *A Shakespeare Companion, 1564–1964,* was the first comprehensive encyclopedia on the subject to appear and it was brought up to date and published in a handy paperback edition in the 400th anniversary year of Shakespeare's birth. It is a masterly work, written with extraordinary clarity and conciseness, and has a helpful system of cross-references, as well as a comprehensive bibliography.

A shorter book, but often useful, is Arthur E. Barker's *A Shakespeare Commentary.* This presents complete information on the sources of the plots, place-names, characters, words, and genealogies, with a fold-in diagram of the characters in the history plays set out in a royal family tree.

Granger's Index to Poetry, edited by Raymond J. Dixon, contains a title and first-line index, an author index, and a subject index. By using these the source of a Shakespeare quotation may be traced because where there is uncertainty about the exact wording, the subject index may be used. Because of its arrangement, it also contains a convenient guide to quotable passages from each of the plays. L. L. M. Marsden's *Shakespearean Quotations in Everyday Use,* published in 1964 is a small book, well printed, with the quotations spread across the page, instead of being contained within double columns, but naturally highly selective.

Specialized dictionaries include A. F. Falconer's *A Glossary of Shakespeare's Sea and Naval Terms Including Gunnery,* which is arranged in a sensible alphabetical sequence by main word, with the quotation and the source printed under this heading. There is also the lexicographer Eric Partridge's *Shakespeare's Bawdy,* which includes an essay by the author as well as a full glossary.

CHAPTER 5

Shakespeare's Sources

FAR and away the most complete and comprehensive account of this subject is contained in the 6 volumes of Professor Geoffrey Bullough's *Narrative and Dramatic Sources of Shakespeare*. Originally planned to be complete in 5 volumes, this work has been appearing at intervals over the past 10 years, and another volume is promised. The author explains his purpose thus: "The work . . . will assemble what the editor believes to be the chief narrative and dramatic sources and analogues of Shakespeare's plays and poems so as to assist the reader who, not being a specialist, wishes to explore the working of Shakespeare's mind." Volume 1 covers the early comedies (*Comedy of Errors, Taming of the Shrew, Two Gentlemen of Verona, Midsummer Night's Dream, Love's Labour's Lost, Merchant of Venice*), the Poems, and *Romeo and Juliet*. Volume 2 takes in the comedies from 1597 to 1603 (*Merry Wives of Windsor, Much Ado About Nothing, As You Like It, Twelfth Night, All's Well That Ends Well* and *Measure for Measure*). Volume 3 the earlier English history plays (*Henry VI, Richard III* and *Richard II*). Volume 4 the later English history plays (*King John, Henry IV, Henry V, Henry VIII*). Volume 5 the Roman plays (*Julius Caesar, Antony and Cleopatra, Coriolanus*). Volume 6 other "Classical" plays (*Titus Andronicus, Troilus and Cressida, Timon of Athens* and *Pericles, Prince of Tyre*). The arrangement is thus described:

> In the introduction to each play, after a brief discussion of the date of composition in which E. K. Chambers's chronology is usually followed, the general relationship of the play to the sources and analogues available to the dramatist is described, and quotations are often given from analogues which cannot be edited fully.

The *Taming of the Shrew*, for instance, is dealt with as follows. First, the introduction in which the Induction and Sly theme is considered, then the Petruchio–Katharina story and then the Bianca plot. Next is Source I: "*The Taming of the Shrew: a pleasant conceited Historie*. As it was sundry times acted by the Right Honorable the Earle of Pembrook his servants, 1594"—and the text of this play. II, Analogue: "From S. Goulart: Thrésor d'histoires admirables et memorables, translated by Edward Grimeston, 1607". And, finally, III, Source: "*Supposes*, by George Gascoigne, 1566", text complete. As the editor modestly claims, these volumes constitute a veritable "anthology of Elizabethan reading". He says: "This work was begun in the conviction that Shakespeare was essentially a poet *in the theatre* . . . [a theme that we have noted already several times] and that a full appreciation must relate his imagery, rhythms and ideas to the dramatic handling of the stories and personages as he re-made them."

As T. W. Baldwin showed in his exhaustive *Shakespeare's Small Latine and Lesse Greeke*, published in 2 volumes in Urbana, the education Shakespeare received at his grammar school in Stratford would have equipped him with a fair knowledge of Latin, and his copy of Ovid's *Metamorphoses* may indeed be in the British Museum Library. Scholars are also of the opinion that he knew French and Italian reasonably well. An excellent little book on his classical background is J. A. K. Thomson's *Shakespeare and the Classics* in which he reminds the reader that "there were other ways in which some knowledge of Greece and Rome was impressed upon the most illiterate Elizabethan. There was an almost continuous succession of masques, shows, revels, processions, royal progresses and the like, in each of which there was sure to be one or more characters from ancient history and mythology"—such as Hercules, Atlas, Fortune, Mercury, Jove, Juno as well as nymphs and satyrs, Greeks and Trojans, and so on. The classical world was very much in the mind and sight of the bystander in Elizabethan London. The philosophy of Rome that pervaded Elizabethan thought is discussed in H. B. Charlton's book *The Senecan Tradition in Renaissance Tragedy*. A most useful handbook is *Shakespeare's Plutarch*, edited by T. J. B. Spencer, in which the lives of Julius Caesar, Brutus, Marcus Antonius, and Coriolanus in the translation of Sir Thomas North are edited with an introduction, glossary, and parallel passages from Shakespeare's plays.

Professor Spencer points out some interesting facts that Shakespeare appreciated North's language and adapted many of his best passages for his own dramatic purposes; that he did this when he was at the height of his powers; and that he also versified passages of only average merit, and, of course, he invented whenever North did not give him the situations he wanted. He points out that the edition of North available to Shakespeare was a cumbersome great folio—not the kind of book, like his *Ovid*, easily taken from place to place. The age of Elizabeth was a great time for the translator, as, indeed, is our own age, and a study of this of some value is F. O. Matthiessen's *Translation: an Elizabethan art*.

Gilbert Highet's well-known *The Classical Tradition* has a chapter on 'Shakespeare's classics' in which he writes: "There is no doubt that Shakespeare was deeply and valuably influenced by Greek and Latin culture. The problem is to define how that influence reached him, and how it affected his poetry."

Professor Abbie Findlay Potts, in *Shakespeare and the Faerie Queene*, has written a scholarly book to trace the influence of Edmund Spenser's *Faerie Queene*, which began to appear in 1591, on the work of Shakespeare: "the argument for Shakespeare's knowledge and use of Spenser's *Faerie Queene* in a series of plays beginning with *Much Ado About Nothing* gains force when we study the very different ethical constituent of the plays that precede it, especially the ones mentioned by Francis Meres in 1598."

Raphael Holinshed, who died around 1580, used to preside over the manor court at Packwood near Stratford, so lived not far from Shakespeare during the poet's youth. His famous *Chronicles of England, Scotland and Ireland* were not all his own work, the Scottish parts being mainly a translation of Boece's *Scotorum*

Historae, and the Irish parts were written by Richard Stanyhurst and Edward Campion. But the world knows the work as Holinshed's *Chronicles*, and the edition Shakespeare probably used was published in 1587. A. and J. Nicoll's *Holinshed's Chronicle as Used in Shakespeare's Plays* is the beginning of modern inquiry into the extent of Shakespeare's use of sources in the writing of his *Age of Kings* plays. Professor Bullough writes: "until recently editors underestimated Shakespeare's attention to authorities and assumed he depended almost entirely on Holinshed. Those days are past. . . ." Holinshed followed a long tradition of chronicle writing, and many of the earlier medieval chronicles were made available in printed editions by Caxton and others; these Shakespeare probably read. Tudor histories such as Edward Hall's *The Union of the Two Noble and Illustre Families of Lancastre and York* were also likely to have been used by him. E. M. W. Tillyard's *Shakespeare's History Plays* is one of the best introductions. Another aspect of the matter is studies in C. W. Scott-Giles's book *Shakespeare's Heraldry*.

Much thought has been given to the range of books Shakespeare is likely to have read, and Professor Bullough has been busy editing and republishing a good number of these. In Victorian times the grandson of William Hazlitt, William Carew Hazlitt, a barrister, made a collection of the "plays, romances, novels, poems and histories employed by Shakespeare in the composition of his works" which he published in 6 volumes, a collection not easily come by nowadays. Kenneth Muir complained in his *Shakespeare's Sources* that he had waited many years for someone to deal adequately with the subject before setting down to writing his own book. It is in 2 volumes and is the handiest available work on the subject. Volume 1 deals with the comedies and tragedies and vol. 2 with the histories. The author writes that "detailed study of the sources of individual plays may contribute to our understanding of Shakespeare as a dramatist". A most attractive and valuable chart at the end of vol. 1 sets out the sources used for each of the plays dealt with in that volume; for *Midsummer Night's Dream* Shakespeare made use of no fewer then eight different sources. The way in which he wove these into his own drama, and modified them to suit his purposes, is of the utmost interest.

A source book for a study of Shakespeare's sources is the volume on the *Elizabethan Age and After* in E. A. Baker's monumental *History of the English Novel*, and another such study, though written with a more general purpose, is L. B. Wright's *Middle-class Culture in Elizabethan England*.

In his edition of *Merchant of Venice*, W. Moelwyn Merchant draws attention to the many biblical references which occur throughout the play, and the subject is treated at length in R. S. H. Noble's *Shakespeare's Biblical Knowledge and Use of the Book of Common Prayer*. V. K. Whitaker, in his *Shakespeare's Use of Learning: the growth of his mind and art*, widens the field from the Bible to consider secular learning. Shakespeare obviously never lost an opportunity of "improving his mind", and documents discovered in the Public Record Office indicate that when he was writing *Henry V* he was lodging with a French Huguenot family in London whose conversation was no doubt helpful to him in the composition of the French scenes in that play. W. H. D. Rouse edited *Shakespeare's Ovid, Golding's Translation of the Metamorphoses*, and G. C. Taylor has studied *Shakespeare's Debt to Montaigne*. Another source not to be neglected is folk tradition, and this has been considered by Janet Spens in her *Essay on Shakespeare's Relation to Tradition*.

Most modern editions of the plays give a short account of the source material likely to have been used by Shakespeare. A ready guide to this material is to be found in F. E. Halliday's already-mentioned *Shakespeare Companion, 1564–1964*, in which each of the plays fits into the alphabetical arrangement and is treated under a number of headings—written, performed, published, sources, stage history. The paragraph headed "sources" gives a summary of the relevant information. The Arden Shakespeare has the most detailed information, often reprinting some of the source material.

Sister Miriam Joseph's *Shakespeare's Use of the Arts of Language* shows the influence of the syllabus taught in the grammar schools of his time, and tabulates passages to be found in works of Tudor logic and rhetoric.

Finally, a bibliography, although unfortunately not very up to date, is Selma Guttman's *The Foreign Sources of Shakespeare's Works: an annotated bibliography of the commentary written on this subject between 1904 and 1940, together with lists of certain translations available to Shakespeare*, New York, 1947.

CHAPTER 6

Literary Criticism

THERE is apparently no end to the books which can be written about Shakespeare's works; his words go to the critics' heads like wine. On the shelves of even quite small public libraries hundreds of books by the literary pundits confront the inquiring reader. Where is he to start? Where is he to stop? How can he make the best use of the vast array of volumes? What is he seeking—a deeper understanding of the plays?—an entrée into the subtle recesses of the academic mind?—the fascination of a prolonged and often entertaining argument, the stuff of which is the stuff of life itself? What of the inexpert student, confronted with long reading lists, reeling with the wit and reasoning of a lecturer deeply versed in the ways of the literary schools? All the student asks is that he may know what to say, so that in his answers to examination questions he does not appear an ass. And yet it all begins by plain men reading the plays, or seeing them produced, and being so stimulated by them that a train of thought is set going, the intellect is stirred to indefatigable life, so that the more the plays are studied the more there is to say about them—so, what advice has the librarian to offer?

Let us begin with honest Dr. Johnson. Sir Walter Raleigh, the twentieth-century Sir Walter, that is, selected and set forth essays and notes by *Johnson on Shakespeare* in a handy little volume first published in 1908. An attractive recent volume, *A Johnson Collection*, edited with notes by F. R. Miles, contains Johnson's *Proposals for Printing the Dramatic Works of William Shakespeare* and his *Preface to Shakespeare*. This *Preface* and selections from the notes on the plays from Johnson's edition of the works are also printed in the handsome Reynard Library edition of John-son's *Poetry and Prose*, edited by Mona Wilson. Johnson, in his blunt English way, gives the reason for his critical labours on Shakespeare thus: "But because human judgement, although it be gradually gaining upon certainty, never becomes infallible; and approbation, though long continued, may yet be only the appro-bation of prejudice or fashion; it is proper to inquire by what peculiarities of excellence Shakespeare has gained and kept the favour of his countrymen." He also has a very useful piece of advice to the student: "He that will understand *Shakespeare*, must not be content to study him in the closet, he must look for his meaning sometimes among the sports of the field, and sometimes among the manufactures of the shop." As Raleigh says, Johnson is "the most punctiliously truthful of all English writers", and it is with his few pages of the *Proposals* and the *Preface* that all who wish to learn more about Shakespeare should begin. "*Shake-speare*," wrote Johnson, "whether life or nature be his subject, shews plainly, that he has seen with his own eyes; he gives the image which he receives, not weakened or distorted by the inter-vention of any other mind; the ignorant feel his representations to be just, and the learned see that they are compleat."

Some 80 years after the work of Johnson came Samuel Taylor Coleridge's *Shakespearean Criticism* which has been edited by T. M. Raysor in 2 volumes. "In the history of English literary criticism", writes the Professor, "there is no work which surpasses in interest Coleridge's lectures upon Shakespeare." Professor Raysor's introduction to Coleridge's criticism is itself a masterly study of some of the main themes of Shakespearean study. Despite its bulk, Coleridge's work is fragmentary, consisting of marginalia, notes from manuscripts, lecture notes, and reports of lecture series delivered from time to time between 1808 and 1819. Yet, despite the lack of any careful plan, or logical development, the fragments present a body of work which the learned are happy continually to study.

Coleridge notes two great causes of false criticism: "the great pleasure we feel in being told of the knowledge we possess, rather than the ignorance we suffer", and "a second permanent cause of false criticism is connected with the habit of not taking the trouble to think: it is the custom which some people have established of judging books by books". Coleridge exemplifies this:

A friend of mine had seen it stated somewhere, or heard it said, that Shakespeare had not made Constance, in *King John*, speak the language of nature, when she exclaims on the loss of Arthur,

> Grief fills the room up of my absent child,
> Lies in his bed, walks up and down with me;
> Puts on his pretty looks, repeats his words,
> Remembers me of all his gracious parts,
> Stuffs out his vacant garments with his form:
> Then have I reason to be fond of grief.

(*King John*, Act iii, Scene 4.)

Within three months after he had repeated this opinion (not thinking for himself) that these lines were out of nature, my friend died. I called upon his mother, an affectionate, but ignorant woman, who had scarcely heard the name of Shakespeare, much less read any of his plays. Like Philip, I endeavoured to console her, and among other things I told her, in the anguish of her sorrow, that she seemed to be as fond of grief as she had been of her son. What was her reply? Almost a prose parody on the very language of Shakespeare—the same thoughts in nearly the same words, but with a different arrangement. An attestation like this is worth a thousand criticisms.

Coleridge can retain his critical powers while at the same time insisting that "the Englishman who without reverence, who without a proud and affectionate reverence, can utter the name of Shakespeare, stands disqualified of the office". And, "it has been and it still remains my object to prove that in all points from the most important to the most minute, the judgement of Shakespeare is commensurate with his genius—nay, that his genius reveals itself in his judgement, as in its most exalted form".

No man can have read the works of Shakespeare with more absorption than John Keats, who wrote: "Thank God I can read, and perhaps understand Shakespeare to his very depths". Keats never wrote about him as a critic. As John Middleton Murry explains in his *Keats and Shakespeare: a study of Keats' poetic life from 1816 to 1820*; "The most intimate motion of Keats' inward life gradually revealed itself to me as a motion of loyalty to Shakespeare the man." The *Letters* of John Keats contain many references to Shakespeare, such as "at once it struck me what quality went to form a man of achievement, especially in literature, and which Shakespeare possessed so enormously—I mean Negative Capability, that is, when a man is capable of being in uncertainties, mysteries, doubts, without any irritable reaching after fact and reason. . . ."

It is in the twentieth century that writing about Shakespeare has become almost an industry, and it is now my task to offer some guidance on how to find out about Shakespeare from this enormous quantity of material. First let it be said that at the beginning of the century, A. C. Bradley, then Professor of Poetry at Oxford University, published *Shakespearean Tragedy*, an analysis of *Othello*, *Lear*, *Hamlet*, and *Macbeth*, which earned a terrific acclaim, then suffered something of an eclipse, but is now returning to favour. There can be few who have studied Shakespeare who have not approached his work. Second, let a brief mention be made of Edward Dowden's *Shakspere: a critical study of his mind and art*, published in 1889, which began a method much followed in our times: "The attempt made in this volume to connect the study of Shakespeare's works with an inquiry after the personality of the writer, and to observe, as far as is possible, in its several stages, the growth of his intellect and character from youth to full maturity, distinguishes the work from the greater number of preceding criticisms of Shakespeare." It should also be noted that Dowden insists on Shakespeare's "resolute fidelity to the fact".

The various approaches to Shakespeare in the works of modern critics are explained with wonderful clarity by Helen Gardner in her essay *Shakespeare and the Age of Eliot* which first appeared in *The Times Literary Supplement* for 23 April 1964, the issue commemorating the 400th anniversary of his birth. She says that for all that has been published "there has not emerged a magisterial work. There is no single critic of the last fifty years who can take his place beside Johnson, Coleridge or Bradley". She quotes T. S. Eliot's remark about the life of a poet being "to transmute his personal and private agonies into something rich and strange, something universal and impersonal" and "the great poet in writing himself is writing his times". She demonstrates that Eliot's ideas expressed in his literary criticism led critics to examine what was symbolized by Shakespeare's characters in the "obscure and complicated feelings" of the author. She singles out Wilson Knight as the critic who followed Eliot most effectively, searching for patterns of imagery and attempting to trace themes and problems in the plays; but she reminds the reader that Shakespeare's supreme gift is "his power to endow the persons of his dramas with independent life, the boundless generosity and charity of his imagination that gives to even the basest, or the most ridiculous, or the feeblest of the beings that people his imaginative world the gift of expression and the right to speak in their own persons." Thus the plays are not for the study but for the stage, and all the problems then arise of the actors' interpretations of the characters, which Eliot worried about. Helen Gardner points out that the psychological awareness which has preoccupied man in this century puts great stress on the inner world of a man, of what it is like to be such and such a person, rather than what such and such a person looks like from the outside—so there has been a revival in our age of allegory, and a distaste for comedy, because we cannot bear to think our inner lives are laughable in any way. Thinking of works of art as symbols has led to the disregard of large-scale works, impossible to fit into a tight symbolic scheme.

Dr. Gardner plainly thinks that these tendencies were to be deplored, and quotes a passage from Mary Lascelles's often praised book on *Measure for Measure*:

> For all its disadvantages, however; for all the perils of misunderstanding with which it is beset; the study of characters in their relations with one another—here, conditioned by the given story, there, developing free of it—remains the right approach; and its alternative, a pursuit of phantoms; of inner and innermost meanings derived from word or phrase that has been isolated from its context, of an intention not demonstrably the dramatist's.

Few scholars have the patience to explain to the uninitiated what their subject is all about from the simple fundamentals upwards, but in the field of Shakespeare studies we have reason to be grateful to the late Professor of English Literature at the University of Aberdeen, George Ian Duthie, whose short book *Shakespeare* is deservedly frequently reprinted. He recommends three books to the beginner. These are E. K. Chambers's *Shakespeare: a survey*, which consists of short introductions to the plays for ordinary readers, written in the years 1904–8 but not collected into 1 volume until 1925; J. Dover Wilson's *The Essential Shakespeare*; and G. B. Harrison's *Introducing Shakespeare*, which is a superb achievement, compressing into eight short chapters the essence of all that is involved in the study of Shakespeare.

To return to Professor Duthie's book, which he says is "addressed primarily to the non-specialist" and "as far as the bulk of the book is concerned, it might well have been entitled 'The order theme in Shakespeare' ". Duthie gives ample evidence that this theme is the most persistent of all themes throughout Shakespeare's work, and it would appear to me that this is why there has been such an enormous success for the plays of Shakespeare on screen and television, because this theme of order so mightily preoccupies our age for we feel we may have lost it for ever. Professor Duthie recommends three books which explain the idea of order for the Elizabethans—Professor Lovejoy's *The Great Chain of Being*, Dr. Tillyard's *Elizabethan World Picture*, and Professor Spencer's *Shakespeare and the Nature of Man*. The universe was thought to be ordered either as a great chain of being, hieratically arranged, with hierarchies within hierarchies, or as a set of parallel planes, with correspondences between those of similar place in each plane, or as a dance to music, harmonious and rhythmic movement. Shatter the order, and what is man left with but himself—"a unique, independent being, self-reliant, individualistic" but, as Shakespeare reminds us over and over again, liable to be overcome, as by

> appetite, an universal wolf . . .
> Must make perforce an universal prey,
> And last eat up himself.

The shattering of the universal order was taking place in Shake-

speare's time, Duthie insists: "It is essential to a right understanding of Shakespeare to realise that the fundamental antithesis
between order and disorder is ubiquitous in his work." The disorder is studied very often in characters with disordered minds,
for, as Dr. Tillyard explains, to the Elizabethans the brain was

> like the body . . . divided into a triple hierarchy. The lowest contained
> the five senses. The middle contained first the common sense, which
> received and summarised the reports of the five senses, second the fancy,
> and third the memory. This middle area supplied the materials for the
> highest to work on. The highest contained the supreme human faculty,
> the reason, by which man is separated from the beasts and allied to God
> and the angels, with its two parts, the understanding (or wit) and the will.

Disturbance of mental order, of course, very often leads to
comedy, rather than the tragedy which follows the shattering of
the cosmic order. Professor Duthie describes also the method of
imaginative interpretation used by G. Wilson Knight, who says
that Shakespeare is concerned with values, defined as "those
positive qualities in man, those directions taken by human action,
which to the imaginative understanding clearly receive high poetic
honours throughout in Shakespeare". These values are assailed by
negations, love by hate, order by disorder, and so on. He quotes
the criticism of this method made by L. C. Knights in his book
Explorations: "a preoccupation with imagery and symbols, unless
minutely controlled by a sensitive intelligence directed upon the
text, can lead to abstractions almost as dangerous as does a preoccupation with character"—this last preoccupation, of course,
being the fault which the critics of the Eliot–Knight school found
with A. C. Bradley's *Shakespearean Tragedy*. Duthie devotes a
long chapter to an examination of the method of Wilson Knight,
using *Troilus and Cressida* as an example. His final three chapters
discuss the history plays, tragedy, and the last plays, where he
commends the view of E. M. W. Tillyard expressed in his book
Shakespeare's Last Plays: "One of Shakespeare's main concerns
in his last plays, whether deliberately taken up or fortuitously
drifted into, was to develop the final phase of the tragic pattern."

This then is how two modern scholars review the work of
Shakespearean criticism of the past 50 years. Using the pattern of

development which they have outlined, let me now refer to the individual works of the critics they name, and those of others who follow their leads.

T. S. Eliot's criticism of Shakespeare is contained in a few essays contained in his book *Elizabethan Essays* notably 'Shakespeare and the Stoicism of Seneca,' in which he makes such typically enigmatic comments as: "The influence of Seneca is much more apparent in the Elizabethan drama than it is in the plays of Seneca", "I am used to having cosmic significances, which I never suspected, extracted from my work". Eliot's essay *Hamlet* contains the influential sentence: "The only way of expressing emotion in the form of art is by finding an 'objective correlative'; in other words, a set of objects, a situation, a chain of events which shall be the formula of that *particular* emotion; such that when the external facts, which must terminate in sensory experience, are given, the emotion is immediately evoked." References to Shakespeare in other essays occur from time to time in Eliot's work, but his most insistent comment is that "if any one of Shakespeare's plays were omitted we should not be able to understand the rest as well as we do".

The Shakespearean criticism of G. Wilson Knight extends over 7 volumes, entitled *The Wheel of Fire, The Imperial Theme, The Shakespearean Tempest, The Olive and the Sword, The Crown of Life, The Mutual Flame,* and *The Sovereign Flower.* The prefatory note to the third edition of *The Shakespearean Tempest* contains a chart of Shakespeare's dramatic universe, "devised to form a kind of *vade mecum* for the Shakespearean expert". This chart is accompanied by a discussion of Duthie's comments in his book *Shakespeare* on Knight's interpretation of *Troilus and Cressida*, and thus the whole preface is a useful introduction to the method of spatial symbolic interpretation employed by Knight in his 7 volumes: "the progress of man", he writes, "is as the progress of creation: from chaos and tempest to light and music. And this sequence is everywhere welded into the Shakespearean imagination." Few critics quote so copiously from the plays as Professor Knight and none have so consistently applied a method of interpretation to the whole of Shakespeare's works. A chapter from *The Sovereign Flower*, entitled 'The Shakespearean Integrity, and reprinted in a shortened version in Anne Ridler's selection of *Shakespeare Criticism, 1935–1960*, is an excellent summary of Shakespeare's qualities, and the final paragraph claims that the organic harmony of his work resembles rather the works of nature than the works of man.

Those who follow the genealogy of ideas will be interested in the 1951 prefatory note which Knight wrote to his *The Imperial Theme*. He sees his work as in the tradition of A. C. Bradley, which he says "is too often wrongly supposed to have been limited to the *minutiae* of characterisation". He also acknowledges his indebtedness to the thought of Middleton Murry and emphasizes his "will to find in great literature significances that may best, to challenge the opposition and avoid all misunderstanding, be called 'mystical' ". Yet he diverges from Murry in his determination to be precise in his handling of imagery and symbol, for Murry feared a new dogmatism in this exact approach. Wilson Knight also denies that he has derived any ideas from the work of Caroline Spurgeon, pointing out that her first book, *Leading Motives in the Imagery of Shakespeare Tragedies* was published in the same year as his *Wheel of Fire*.

G. B. Harrison's invaluable *Introducing Shakespeare*, already referred to, has a chapter on the modern approach to Shakespeare. In this he says that students of Shakespeare today are interested mainly in three kinds of study: the scholarly (which is concerned with textual problems and Elizabethan stage conditions—see chapters 5 and 6 of this book); the literary; and the dramatic. All three approaches, he says, meet in the work of Harley Granville-Barker, whose magnificent set of *Prefaces to Shakespeare*, available collected in 2 volumes, must now be mentioned. Granville-Barker began his theatrical career as a playwright, one of his plays achieving notoriety by being banned by the censor. His most influential work was as a producer at the Savoy Theatre. Incredible as it may seem now, Shakespeare's plays were thought to be unactable in those days, and all kinds of gimmicks were introduced into the productions, such as fountains with real goldfish on the stage in *Antony and Cleopatra*. Granville-Barker had a built up apron-stage, similar to that of Shakespeare's own day, formalized the scenery, and used the text as Shakespeare wrote it without any cuts. He only produced three of the plays before the First World War broke out in 1914, and he never resumed his work in the theatre. But from 1927 onwards he published his *Prefaces*, which had all the authority of a playwright and producer as well as of the literary scholar. The last 3 volumes are devoted to one play each, *Hamlet* in vol. 3; *Othello* in vol. 4, and *Coriolanus* in vol. 5. The first volume studies *Love's Labour's Lost*, *Julius Caesar*, and *King Lear*, and vol. 2 *Romeo and Juliet*, *Merchant of Venice*, *Antony and Cleopatra* and *Cymbeline*.

The principal trends in Shakespearean scholarship are examined by Professor Kenneth Muir in his chapter, entitled 'Changing interpretations of Shakespeare', which, although reviewing the work of major critics from the seventeenth century onwards, concentrates mainly on those of the last 50 years (in *The Age of Shakespeare*, which is the second volume of the series of Pelican guides to English literature edited by Professor Boris Ford).

The *Cambridge Quarterly* has a long paper by J. M. Newton in the Spring 1966 issue with the provocative title of '*Scrutiny's* failure with Shakespeare'—*Scrutiny*, of course, being the journal edited with such *éclat* by F. R. Leavis of Downing College. This essay, I think, marks a significant turn in the critical tide.

There are a vast number of much-read books of criticism, commentary, and interpretation which I propose to divide into eight types, as follows:

1. General studies.
2. Interpretative and pyschological studies.
3. Studies of the comedies.
4. Studies of the tragedies.
5. Studies of the histories and Roman plays.
6. Studies of the later plays.
7. Studies of character in the plays.
8. Tales from Shakespeare's plays.

1. *General Studies*

One of the most frequently quoted writers is John Middleton Murry, whose *Shakespeare* was published in the thirties and reissued in 1954, with a foreword by the author. Murry was not an academic, but he was a literary critic of the very highest class, and like all men of quality he was able to take a look at himself. Correcting a view he had expressed in the first edition of his book, he writes in his foreword to the second edition: "it was preposterous of me to say that Shakespeare was out of his depth, when the evidence stares me in the face that I was out of mine." There are notable essays on Shakespeare in Murry's two published collections of literary criticism, entitled *Countries of the Mind*, first and second series.

George Bernard Shaw was no very great admirer of the academic mind, and was deeply jealous of Shakespeare's hold over the best actors and actresses, notably Miss Ellen Terry, when he was anxious to secure their services in the performance of his own plays. Despite such outbursts as "Shakespeare is to me one of the towers of the Bastille, and down he must come"; and "With the single exception of Homer, there is no eminent writer, not even Sir Walter Scott, whom I can despise so entirely as I despise Shakespeare when I measure my mind against his", Shaw's accounts of Shakespeare performances in the *Saturday Review* were notable not only for the wit and fluency of his writing but for the percipience of his dramatic criticism. In his admirable collection *Shaw on Shakespeare*, Mr. Edwin Wilson has collected some of these pieces and organized them, together with excerpts from Shaw's letters and the prefaces he wrote to his own plays, into a body of criticism, arranged first, play by play, then giving opinions on such topics as 'Shakespeare the man' and interpreters like Shaw's *bête-noir*, Henry Irving, of whom he writes: "He had really only one part; and that part was the part of Irving. . . . The Merchant of Venice became the Martyrdom of Irving, which was, it must be confessed, far finer than the Tricking of Shylock . . . he had no power of adapting himself to an author's conception. . . ."

Another world, outside the accepted Western tradition, is represented in K. R. Srinivasa Iyengar's book *Shakespeare: his work and his art* which is a thorough and complete introduction, sorting out the significant and the trivial in a way which is refreshing.

Margaret Webster's book *Shakespeare To-day* is another non-academic study written from much experience as a producer, and that not always of the usual kind, for, although she has put on Shakespeare at Stratford in the Memorial Theatre, she has also taken a "Shakespeare on Wheels" company about the United States, playing in forty-four states over a period of 3 years. The book is all the more interesting because she is so aware of the tensions of modern society and writes: "Shakespeare seems to have been moving steadily nearer to this terrible confrontation between his tragic 'heroes' and the cosmic forces beyond mortal knowledge", which in these days of burning racial hatreds and the balance of nuclear power makes Shakespeare truly a contemporary of ours.

Two volumes published to commemorate the 400th anniversary of Shakespeare's birth contain studies of a good many of the plays by modern critics. They are *Shakespeare, 1564–1964*, edited by Edward A. Bloom, and *Shakespeare 400*, edited by James G. McManaway.

D. A. Traversi, in his *An Approach to Shakespeare*, examines the recurrent words, phrases, images, and themes, tracing a symbolic pattern underlying the development in the plays themselves, thus attempting to set Shakespeare's work within a framework of artistic unity, a unity which most modern critics insist existed.

John Wain says of his intentions regarding his *Living World of Shakespeare*: "The people I am concerned with are those who fill the theatres in London and Stratford . . . where Shakespeare's plays are staged; and the actors and (dare I add?) producers responsible for that staging; and the radio and television staff who adapt Shakespeare to their own media now and again; and the amateur dramatic societies who undertake Shakespearean productions in village halls." The book, however, has more in common with the studies of the academics than with the world of the average playgoer.

No general introduction can be of more value to the beginner than Alfred Harbage's *William Shakespeare: a reader's guide*. The author has used his great learning to help the newcomer, writing:

> Many of us have observed in our travels that the best guides are often those who assert themselves least. . . . I aspire in this book to be a good guide, but I am not allowed to be taciturn. . . . I believe that a guide may be warm in his testimony, providing he sticks to particulars. My book owes much to Shakespearean criticism, and it seems churlish to say that it is intended in part to defend readers from criticism. A good safeguard in reading Shakespeare criticism is to read it extensively, until one grows aware of its collaborative nature and of how extreme positions are cancelled out. Better still, of course, is close knowledge of the works themselves, so that one can distinguish between critical opinions based on observation and those based on divination.

Then he goes on with these truly illuminating words: "The object of my book is to induce a noticing mood, to encourage attentive reading, and to save the fundamental, the conspicuous, the important from being dismissed as elementary." Under four headings, namely 'Mastery achieved', 'Infinite variety', 'Death and poetry', and 'Valediction', he takes the reader carefully through fourteen of the most well-known plays, act by act, often scene by scene. The first section of the book contains a masterly summary of the words, the lines, and the script, which more familiarly may be referred to as figures of speech, grammar, prosody, and what the Elizabethans called "the book of the play". This section contains some short bibliographies.

One of Peter Alexander's earliest books on Shakespeare, published before the Second World War, *Shakespeare's Life and Art*, sets out a useful short commentary on each of the plays, with the essential minimum of reference to the events of Shakespeare's life and the ways of the Elizabethan stage and publisher. It is proper to note that, despite the favour he finds at Mr. Louis Mander's hands, Nicholas Rowe is discredited by Professor Alexander. In fact most of the eighteenth-century pundits, with the exception of Dr. Johnson, are shown to have written with extraordinary prejudice and lack of balance, which is surprising for the exemplars of an age of enlightenment and reason. The opinions of David Hume are quite remarkable for their purblind contempt; namely that Shakespeare was born in a rude age, educated in the lowest manner, gained no instruction from books, wrote his plays for the least refined and most ignorant of his contemporaries, having no artistic ideals, his chief aim being financial gain. One can never, after reading this, have very much confidence in the conclusions of the great David's urbane reason.

John Garrett is the editor of two books of texts and lectures delivered at the Shakespeare Memorial Theatre's Summer Schools, where notable authorities, like Helen Gardner, addressed themselves to the task of helping teachers to refresh their understanding of the plays the better to instruct their charges. These books are entitled *Talking about Shakespeare* and *More Talking about Shakespeare*, and contain a wide variety of studies on the plays and their interpretation, and on other themes.

When one great poet writes about another, the result will always be interesting, though not always readily acceptable. Edith Sitwell's *A Notebook of William Shakespeare*, is what she herself called "a running commentary" on certain aspects of Shakespeare. This consists of quotations from scholars and from other writers whose writings contain passages that Dame Edith thought appropriate to her purpose. She has added her own opinions and in addition provides studies of her own on *Macbeth*, *King Lear* and *Othello*. It is a fascinating book, an enriching experience to read, but one regrets that it has not been more lavishly produced, with illustrations, or at least on good paper with an adventurous type face.

John Masefield's *William Shakespeare* is made up of a series of short chapters, one on each of the plays, taken more or less in the order in which it is maintained they were written. A synopsis of the plot is followed by Masefield's own remarks, always forthright and sometimes not in accord with present-day evaluations, as when he writes of *Titus Andronicus*, "the piece is nearly worthless".

A work by a French scholar that is often praised by English

writers is Henri Fluchère's *Shakespeare: dramaturge élisabéthain,* which has been translated by Guy Hamilton as *Shakespeare* and published with an introduction by T. S. Eliot. The book is in three parts: 'Spirit of the Age', 'Technique', and 'The Themes'.

Logan Pearsall Smith begins his short book *On Reading Shakespeare,* with the guarded sentence: "I am not a Shakespeare scholar, nor am I a constant reader of his plays", but this should not lead the reader to expect he is going to have his time wasted by inexpert maunderings if he reads on. Smith was famous in his time for his accurate scholarship and deep knowledge of the English language. Although out of favour now, because he enjoyed Shakespeare in the study rather than in the theatre, his book is a feast of appreciation of the poetry of the plays. His own style is perhaps somewhat too poetic for our downright time, as when he says he loves best those plays "silvery tinted with the cast of thought".

Mark van Doren's *Shakespeare* has been called a graceful book, and it is certainly more easily read than works of more formal scholarship, which is not to say that the author is not learnedly equipped. Like Shakespeare himself he does not make it obvious where his sympathies lie, but describes the themes of all the plays, and the confrontation of ideas, as in *As You Like It*: "the idea of the simple life has been smiled off the earth and yet here it is smiling back at us from every bough of Arden".

Those who tire of the universal praise of Shakespeare should consider these extracts from a letter printed in the *Annual Register* for 1776:

> The worst of it is that the monster has a party in France; and what is particularly unfortunate, 'twas I that formerly first talked of this Shakespeare;—'twas I that shewed the French some pearls which I found on his enormous dunghill—I little thought that I should help to tread underfoot the crowns of Racine and Corneille, to adorn the head of a buffoon and barbarian.

These words were written by François Arouet, better known as Voltaire, and the remarks that annoyed him were contained in an introduction to a French edition of Shakespeare which said, among other things, that "Shakespeare was the creative deity of the sublime art of dramatic writing; which received at his hands existence and perfection". Voltaire published his thoughts on Shakespeare in his *Lettres philosophiques sur les Anglais.* It is interesting, incidentally, to find him complaining of the entry of English words, like beef-steak, into the French language, a process which still continues, though the French language does not seem to suffer unduly.

Leo Tolstoi, too, has added his powerful disapproval in his essay *Shakespeare and the Drama.*

2. *Interpretative and Psychological Studies*

For sheer intellectual power one of the most absorbing of interpretative studies is contained in Rebecca West's *The Court and the Castle* which she subtitles "a study of the interactions of political and religious ideas in imaginative literature". The first 70 pages of this book are a study of *Hamlet* and some others of Shakespeare's plays concerned with the theme of will, especially the will of those in authority.

The most famous of all the interpretative studies is that by Caroline Spurgeon, *Shakespeare's Imagery and What It Tells Us.* This set in motion a whole new field of research, as the author predicted when she said that the possibilities of developing her ideas relating to Shakespeare's use of imagery had endless scope. On the title-page of her book is the following quotation from *Hamlet*:

> And thus do we of wisdom and of reach,
> With windlasses and with assays of bias,
> By indirections find direction out,

which is a fair clue to her intentions. She writes:

> The novelty of the procedure I am describing is that *all* his images are assembled, sorted, and examined on a systematic basis, the good with the bad, the disagreeable with the pleasant, the coarse with the refined, the attractive with the unattractive, and the poetical with the unpoetical. . . . They are not selected to point or to illustrate any preconceived idea or thesis. . . .

She claims for her method of investigation that "it enables us to get nearer to Shakespeare himself, to his mind, his tastes, his experience, and his deeper thought than does any other single way I know of studying him". Her book is divided into two parts; the first treats of the 'Revelation of the man' and the second of 'The function of the imagery as background and undertone in Shakespeare's art'. Other critics, while acknowledging the range and depth of insight undeniably to be found in her book, have been a little aghast at a method which appears to apply purely mechanical arts of card-indexing analysis to so complex a subject as the verse and prose of Shakespeare's plays. However, the proof of the pudding is in the eating. Those who think that Shakespeare was Bacon, or Marlowe, or someone else, have never attempted to attack the conclusions of this book, and with reason.

In the first part, Caroline Spurgeon puts together a convincing portrait, perhaps a little larger than life, of Shakespeare, composed from her study of his imagery. She sees him as a countryman through and through, his works abounding in imagery from nature and the countryside and from the various sports to be found there. She writes:

> Physical alertness and well-being is but a part of Shakespeare's intense vitality, which goes to make him an almost incredibly sensitive and amazingly observant man. Probably he was a quiet one—he does not like noise—though not it would seem, a dreamer, but practical and watchful, all the time absorbing impressions and movements like a sponge, registering them like a sensitive plate.

For good measure the authoress provides seven charts at the end of her book, illustrating the range and subject of the images used by Shakespeare, comparing these with five contemporary dramatists—Marlowe, Jonson, Chapman, Dekker, and Massinger, and also with Bacon. She also presents diagrammatically the use of certain sets of images in Shakespeare's plays, noting how some sets predominate in one or two of the plays, a valuable clue to the preoccupations which Shakespeare intended to study in those particular plays.

A German scholar, Wolfgang Clemen, has also made a thorough

study in depth of Shakespeare's use of imagery in a book entitled *Development of Shakespeare's Imagery*, which was written at about the same time as Caroline Spurgeon's and has been re-issued since the war. "Every image, every metaphor gains full life and significance only from its context . . . it appears as a cell in the organism of the play, linked with it in many ways. It is the aim of this book to investigate these relations and connections, in order to arrive at a truly organic method of understanding the images." Needless to say these books have stimulated a crowd of papers from other scholars, making use of the methods described, but none of such note as the models they follow. Una Ellis-Fermor has summarized some of the work in her *Some Recent Research in Shakespeare's Imagery*, and Maurice Charney, in his *Shakespeare's Roman Plays*, proceeds by an analysis of the imagery, noting his indebtedness to Cleanth Brooks's work in his well-known *The Well-wrought Urn*. Edward A. Armstrong's *Shakespeare's Imagination: a study of the psychology of association and inspiration* follows the method, and the author has provided some tables of his own devising to present diagrammatically an analysis of "image clusters".

John Bayley, in his *The Characters of Love: a study in the literature of personality*, has written a study which already is being acclaimed as significant for its new perspectives. He writes of his intentions: "The most important thing I hope to show is that an author's success with this theme is closely linked with his attitude towards his own characters—that author, in fact, is best on love who best loves his own creations." Bayley is very critical of much modern criticism of *Othello*, of which he makes a special study, noting the similarity in subject-matter between this play and the domestic novel—the study of private life, domesticity, and daily private living—particularly of G. Wilson Knight and T. S. Eliot. He lets off A. C. Bradley with the comment that he is "less inadequate" than the others.

The theme of wedded love in the plays is studied by Alfred Harbage in his *Shakespeare and the Rival Traditions* of which the author writes: "My aim is to present a new synthesis of the facts about Elizabethan theatres and the contents of Elizabethan plays, as a means of defining Shakespeare's materials and intentions." A method which the reader will appreciate is in the line of the work of Harley Granville-Barker.

The psychoanalysts, of course, have found plenty of material for their theories in Shakespeare's plays, and if one is to believe the literary critics, have written some remarkably foolish books in making use of this material. But one of the books has stood the test of time—*Hamlet and Oedipus* by Dr. Ernest Jones, the biographer and Welsh disciple of Freud. Jones quotes W. F. Trench on the obscurity of the play: "We find it hard, with Shakespeare's help to understand Hamlet: even Shakespeare, perhaps, found it hard to understand him: Hamlet himself finds it impossible to understand himself. Better able than other men to read the hearts and motives of others, he is yet quite unable to read his own." Yet, asks Jones, why does the play continue to have so powerful an effect on the audience if it is so obscure. He insists that it is because the conflict in the heart of the hero is one that is matched in the heart of the spectator. And the theme of the book is that "the explanation of the delay and self frustration exhibited in the endeavour to fulfil his father's demand for vengeance is that to Hamlet the thought of incest and parricide combined is too intolerable to be borne".

3. *Studies of the Comedies*

Perhaps the most readily available general study of the comedies is a book edited by Laurence Lerner, who has described his vocation as poetry. His *Shakespeare's Comedies: an anthology of modern criticism* contains pieces by writers as diverse as Sir Arthur Quiller-Couch (on 'The making of *A Midsummer Night's Dream*') and W. H. Auden (on '*The Merchant of Venice*' and '*Twelfth Night*'). He appends a collection of five short essays on comedy and on Shakespearean comedy by Ben Jonson, George Meredith, Northrop Frye, Simon O. Lesser, and H. B. Charlton. He writes in his own introduction that "For better or worse, it is impossible to stop the flood of Shakespeare criticism". He particularly praises a book by C. L. Barber, a professor of English at Amherst College, entitled *Shakespeare's Festive Comedy: a study of dramatic form and its relation to social custom*. Barber's thesis, briefly, is that Shakespeare expresses in his comedies the "experience of moving to humorous understanding through saturnalian release". He points out that in Elizabethan times the seasonal feasts were "the landmarks framing the cycle of the year" and that "Mirth took form in morris dances, sword dances, wassailings, mock ceremonies of summer kings and queens and of lords of misrule, mummings, disguisings, masques—and a bewildering variety of sports, games, shows and pageants." C. L. Barber traces the analogies between social rituals and dramatic forms in the comedies of Shakespeare. In his illuminating remarks on 'Through release to clarification' he claims that there is a sort of conspiracy of enjoyment between the major characters which is enjoyed by the audience, because in coming to the theatre they too are on holiday, and that the butts in the plays, the malcontents who oppose holiday, are shown to be inadequate, thus "Pleasure becomes the touchstone for judgement of what bars it or is incapable of it". He quotes a telling extract from Bishop Hugh Latimer's sixth sermon before Edward VI, demonstrating how powerful was the hold of the custom of holiday upon the common people:

> I came once myself to a place, riding on a journey homeward from London, and I sent word overnight into the town that I would preach there in the morning because it was a holy day, and me thought it was an holy day's work. The church stood in my way, and I took my horse, and my company, and went thither. I thought I should have found a great company in the church, and when I came there, the church door was fast locked.
>
> I tarried there half an hour and more, at last the key was found and one of the parish comes to me and says: "Sir this is a busy day with us, we cannot hear you, it is Robin Hood's day. The parish are gone abroad to gather for Robin Hood. I pray you let them not."

The chapter headings indicate the scheme of the book. 'Introduction: the saturnalian pattern'; 'Holiday custom and entertainment'; 'Misrule as comedy'; 'Comedy as misrule'; 'Prototypes of festive comedy in a pageant entertainment'; 'The folly of wit and masquerade in *Love's Labour's Lost*'; 'May games and metamorphoses on a midsummer night'; 'The merchant and the Jew of Venice: wealth's communion and an intruder'; 'Rule and misrule in *Henry IV*'; 'the alliance of seriousness and levity in *As You Like It*'; 'Testing courtesy and humanity in *Twelfth Night*'. This book is a masterly treatment of its theme, and the librarian puts in a plea for a readily accessible, preferably paperback edition, to be made available in Great Britain.

> John Russell Brown in his *Shakespeare and His Comedies* writes: However carefree they may seem, there must be some elixir which distinguishes them from the majority of comedies and which bestows longevity upon Shakespeare's jests and fancies; the pleasure that they give whenever they are performed proves that the elixir must be there and, however inappropriate the attempt may seem, the critic must try to isolate and describe it.

And this is what Mr. Brown does try to do, coming to the conclusion:

> All the comedies, early and late, are shaped by consistent and minute judgements; these may be missed on casual reading because they are implicit rather than explicit, but they can be described by analysing some of the simpler means which Shakespeare always used to present them— the repetition of words, images, actions and ideas.

In his book *Comic Characters of Shakespeare* John Palmer considers Berowne, Touchstone, Shylock, Bottom, and Beatrice and Benedict. J. I. M. Stewart, in his *Character and Motive in Shakespeare*, has two illuminating essays on Falstaff: 'Falstaff on Boars Hill' and 'Birth and death of Falstaff'. He complains strongly about those writers who would "give us not merely *Hamlet* without the Prince but the Complete Works without their several *dramatis personae*".

H. B. Charlton's *Shakespearean Comedy* is a work that rarely remains long on the library shelves; the author's approach is summed up, perhaps, in his remarks on the differences between Shakespearean and classical comedy, which he says is conservative, whereas:

> Shakespearian comedy is a more venturesome and a more imaginative undertaking. It does not assume that the conditions and the requisites of man's welfare have been certainly established, and are therefore a sanctity

> only to be safeguarded . . . his heroes (or heroines, to give them the due of their sex) are voyagers in pursuit of a happiness not yet attained, a brave new world wherein man's life may be fuller, his sensations more exquisite and his joys more widespread, more lasting, and so more humane.

This is a theme which is taken up in John Dover Wilson's final book of criticism, his *Shakespeare's Happy Comedies*.

Another theme in the study of comedy is the masque, and this is the subject of Enid Welsford's *The Court Masque*. In her chapter on 'The *Midsummer Night's Dream*' she writes: "The amusement lies in putting the prosy people in charming or unconventional surroundings and laughing at their inadequacy and confusion." She sees the play not as a criticism of life but as a dance, "of which the underlying motif is harmony".

W. H. Auden, in his book *The Dyer's Hand*, has written some telling studies of some of Shakespeare's comedies. In the essay 'Brothers and others' he examines the problems of *The Merchant of Venice*, and the uncompromising nature of his thought is demonstrated throughout: "Belmont would like to believe that men and women are either good or bad by nature, but Shylock and Antonio remind us that this is an illusion: in the real world, no hatred is totally without justification, no love totally innocent. . . ." Auden's book is valuable for the learning he brings to bear on such subjects as usury.

Shakespeare Survey 8 is devoted mainly to essays and studies of the comedies.

The introduction to E. M. W. Tillyard's *Shakespeare's Early Comedies* is a survey of critical writings on the comedies in recent years. The rest of the book is a straightforward account of the following plays: *The Comedy of Errors, The Taming of the Shrew, Two Gentlemen of Verona, Love's Labour's Lost, The Merchant of Venice*.

An American scholar, W. W. Lawrence, wrote a book in 1931 entitled *Shakespeare's Problem Comedies* in which he studied *All's Well That Ends Well, Measure for Measure, Troilus and Cressida*, and *Cymbeline*. His term "problem" to describe these plays has been adapted by other writers, though the more work done on these plays the less of a problem do they become. Lawrence's method is "to base our primary conclusions upon definite and tangible evidence, discarding so far as possible the emotional and moral effect which the plays produce on us to-day". He also maintains, against the trend of most recent criticism, that "there is no evidence that the problem comedies were composed, any more than the more familiar plays, for the gratification of Shakespeare's aesthetic interests, or to give expression to his views on conduct and morality".

Another American scholar, Bertrand Evans, adopts an original approach in his *Shakespeare's Comedies* in which he studies these plays "through one of Shakespeare's notable dramaturgical characteristics—his uses of awareness and control"—that is to say through examining the dramatic effect gained by the method Shakespeare adapts in all of his comedies of allowing the audience to be in possession of knowledge denied to the characters in the plays. Evans asks "How does this play, its action, its people, its world, look from this single point of view?" He takes the plays in the probable order of composition and applies his method with devotion.

Dr. E. M. W. Tillyard, in his *Shakespeare's Problem Plays*, has added *Hamlet* to the trio singled out by W. W. Lawrence, *Troilus and Cressida, All's Well That Ends Well*, and *Measure for Measure*. *Cymbeline* he does not consider. He distinguishes between the four problem plays, saying that about *All's Well* and *Measure for Measure* "there is something radically schizophrenic" but the other two are problem plays because they are about interesting problems. He says the mood of the plays is serious, but not black—they show a strong awareness of evil, without being predominantly pessimistic. Thus the so-called problem comedies are the link with the tragedies.

4. *Studies of the Tragedies*

Far and away the most notable book in this field is A. C. Bradley's *Shakespearean Tragedy* which contains two essays on the substance and the construction of the tragedies and detailed studies of *Hamlet, Othello, King Lear,* and *Macbeth.* He writes: "Our one object will be what, again in a restricted sense, may be called dramatic appreciation; to increase our understanding and enjoyment of these works as dramas." He singles out the prime requisite: "a vivid and intent imagination". The work of comparison, analysis, and dissection is essential, but only as a means to an end: the enrichment of the "imaginative reading or recreation of the drama". The success with which Bradley achieved his objectives may be gauged from the number of times the book has been reprinted; printing after printing has sold out since the first edition appeared in 1904; in every decade new readers have been found, and there is still no sign that the public has tired of it. Bradley's method of character analysis has been subjected to critical attack, but it has survived, and is integral to his purpose. He explains when writing of Hamlet: "the whole story turns upon the peculiar character of the hero. For without this character the whole play would appear sensational and horrible."

A more modern approach to the tragedies is found in John Holloway's *The Story of the Night* in which in addition to the four major tragedies analysed by Bradley, the author includes studies of *Antony and Cleopatra* and *Coriolanus.* He attempts, as he says, tentatively, certainly incompletely and "doubtless in part erroneous", to describe in a chapter entitled 'Shakespearean tragedy and the idea of human sacrifice' a pattern to be found in the tragedies which

> has at its centre a very distinctive role pursued by the protagonist over the whole course of the play: a role which takes him from being cynosure of his society to being estranged from it, and takes him, through a process of increasing alienation, to a point at which what happens to him suggests the expulsion of a scapegoat, or the sacrifice of a victim, or something of both.

Holloway pays tribute in his book to the essay of F. R. Leavis in his book *The Common Pursuit* on the 'Diabolic intellect and the noble hero: or the sentimentalist's Othello' which many others have praised, although he is very critical of the arguments used therein, quoting Leavis's own comment on Bradley that what he wrote "is still a very potent and mischievous influence". However, these chapters belong to the realm of the higher interpretative criticism, and are not for the beginner.

Lily B. Campbell has written some formidably scholarly books about Shakespeare of which *Shakespeare's Tragic Heroes* is certainly one. The book is divided into three parts; the first deals with the purpose and method of tragedy; the second with the moral philosophy of Shakespeare's day; and the third, under the title 'Mirrors of passion', treats of the four major tragedies: *Hamlet*—a tragedy of grief; *Othello*—a tragedy of jealousy; *King Lear*—a tragedy of wrath in old age; *Macbeth*—a study in fear. These four plays are the subject of four essays in C. J. Sisson's *Shakespeare's Tragic Justice*, the motive for his writing them being the way in which the problems of justice, human and divine, can be said to haunt Shakespeare "as it haunted Renaissance Christendom".

John Lawlor writes in *The Tragic Sense in Shakespeare* as follows:

> Shakespeare's very mode of presentation, his characteristic handling of his themes, is in and through the co-existence of opposites—the real and the apparent; man as agent and patient; accident and design in the train of events; natural and supernatural in human affairs; and, finally, the human and the inhuman co-existing in the creature Man.

It is to be remarked in any survey of modern writings on Shakespeare that whereas up until the end of the nineteenth century the major works of the outstanding critics were nearly all concerned with the tragedies, today it is the comedies that have inspired the more lively minds among the literary critics. However, there is one work on the tragedies that cannot be put on one side, and that is H. B. Charlton's *Shakespearean Tragedy*, the published text of the Clark lectures that he gave in Cambridge in 1946–7. In the heart of the world of the new criticism of the period, Charlton proclaimed himself in his first lecture "a devout Bradleyite" and he delivered a broadside at the tenets of those who opposed Bradley's methods. He said of Bradley that he sees the men who move through the plays "as if they were real human beings struggling through a

world which seems in moral substance very much like our own."
These essays have been much read by scholars and students since
they were published, and their popularity gives no sign of fading.
He treats first of what he calls the "apprenticeship pieces", *Titus
Andronicus, Richard III,* and *Richard II*; then "experiment and
interregnum", *Romeo and Juliet, King John,* and *Julius Caesar*; and
finally, a chapter each for *Hamlet, Othello, Macbeth,* and *King
Lear*.

5. *Studies of the Histories and Roman Plays*

Lily B. Campbell's *Shakespeare's 'Histories': mirrors of Elizabethan policy* sides with the critics "who accepted Shakespeare as
a man of Elizabethan England"—a man, that is, immersed in the
life and politics, the ideological struggles and ambitions of the
time, as expressed in its life and literature. She insists that "Shakespeare's plots were clear and sure because he had a definite, fundamental conception of universal law". The first part of this book is
about history, historiography, and politics. The second part considers Shakespeare's political use of history. The authoress studies
the histories from *King John* to *Richard III*, with little reference to
Henry VI or *Henry VIII*. She relates the action of the plays to the
political arguments and rivalries of Elizabeth's reign, showing, for
example, the comparison that was drawn at the time between the
case of Richard II and Elizabeth, which made the deposition scene
so dangerous that it was excluded from most productions of the
play. The deposition of monarchs, or the killing of the King was a
theme which greatly preoccupied Shakespeare, as John F. Danby
shows in his *Shakespeare's Doctrine of Nature: a study of 'King
Lear'*. He also takes his illustrations from *Julius Caesar, Hamlet,
Troilus and Cressida, Othello,* and *Macbeth,* but in *King Lear*
"killing the King is put into a larger framework than Shakespeare
had so far employed. Each of the main actors in the story is
brought into relation with 'nature'. By this each of them acquires
an extra dimension." This "nature" is studied in the early part of
the book in chapters which contrast "benignant nature" to be

found in Lear, with "malignant nature" exemplified in the wicked daughters.

M. M. Reese, in *The Cease of Majesty*, takes the theme of majesty in the histories. Shakespeare was seeking "the ideal social relationship in which King and people were united in a conception of their mutual duty. That is what Shakespeare meant by majesty: a recognition of mutual duty." The first half of the book considers Tudor historians and the philosophic and political ideas of the time, and the second examines the history plays against this background, paying most attention to *Henry VI, Richard II, Richard III, King John, Henry IV*, and *Henry V*.

The author praises D. A. Traversi's *Shakespeare from Richard II to Henry V* and L. C. Knight's *Shakespeare's Politics*.

Shakespeare Survey 10 has a section devoted to the Roman plays, including a review of critical opinion over the past 50 years by J. C. Maxwell. There are two studies of *Titus Andronicus* and one of *Coriolanus*. *Shakespeare Survey 6* is similarly given over to essays on the histories, beginning with a review of critical opinion 1900–51 by Harold Jenkins. A series of studies with the general title *Twentieth Century Views*, edited by Maynard Mack of Yale University, includes a volume on *Shakespeare: the histories, a collection of critical essays*, which is edited by Eugene M. Waith. The editor quotes Professor Charlton as setting the theme of the histories: "The real hero of the English-history play is England." In a useful review of modern criticism of the plays the editor makes the comment: "In spite of all the light that has been thrown on the nature of these plays, it has not ended discussion on what distinguishes a history from any other kind of play." The essays which make up the book are divided into sections, the first tetralogy *Henry VI* and *Richard III* and the second tetralogy *Richard II, Henry IV*, and *Henry V*, with separate chapters for *King John* and *Henry VIII*. The plays are also taken in these groups by Dr. E. M. W. Tillyard in his *Shakespeare's History Plays*. In the first part of his book he writes of the background to the plays under the headings cosmic, historical, literary (dramatic and nondramatic).

J. A. R. Marriott, a well-known historian of the early part of this century, gives in *English History in Shakespeare*, a straightforward account of the political background of the history plays.

A useful reference book to have handy when reading the histories is W. H. Thomson's *Shakespeare's Characters: a historical dictionary*, of which the author writes: "This volume gives an account of all the historical personages appearing as characters, or referred to, in the English Historical Plays and *Macbeth*."

6. *Studies of the Later Plays*

D. A. Traversi writes of these plays in his essay on 'The last plays of Shakespeare' published in *The Age of Shakespeare*, edited by Boris Ford.

> At the heart of each of these plays, present in various forms but clearly responding to a definite continuity of purpose, lies an organic relationship between breakdown and reconstruction, the divisions created in the most intimate bonds (and more especially in the unity of the family) by the action of time and passion and the final healing of these divisions.

Dr. Tillyard's thesis in his elegant book *Shakespeare's Last Plays* is that the romances supplement the tragedies, carry the mood, as it were, a stage further. He distinguishes two major themes of these later plays, which he calls 'the tragic pattern' and 'planes of reality' and indicates how these themes are part of the structure of *Cymbeline*, *Winter's Tale*, and *The Tempest*. He also has a chapter arguing that Shakespeare at this period in his career was greatly "aware of the work of his juniors, Beaumont and Fletcher".

Shakespeare Survey 11 devotes a large part of its contents to a consideration of what are called there 'Shakespeare's romances'— a review of critical opinion from 1900 to 1957 and essays on *The Winter's Tale*, *Cymbeline*, *The Tempest*, and *Two Noble Kinsmen*. Nevill Coghill takes, in his paper, the "six main charges of creaking dramaturgy" made by "Bethell and the Cambridge editors" against *The Winter's Tale* and defends the play against them. He makes the point that "Time is at the heart of the play's mystery".

7. *Studies of Character in the Plays*

To start with the fools, there is a quite exceptionally fascinating account by Leslie Hotson, *Shakespeare's Motley*, in which the author first makes his point that "motley" does not mean "particoloured" and proves that the fool's coat worn in Elizabethan times was woven of threads of different colours, so the motley was a long coat made of a cloth of mixed colour. Needless to say, the answer was in the *Oxford English Dictionary* all the time for all to find, as Hotson acknowledges. He has a long chapter on the man, Robert Arnim, who played Shakespeare's great fools, Touchstone, Feste, and Lear's Fool, and makes the reader wish he had time to read Arnim's own book *Foole Upon Foole*. Robert Hillis Goldsmith suggests in *Wise Fools in Shakespeare* that Erasmus influenced Shakespeare's ideas for the characters of his fools and Enid Welsford in her *The Fool: his social and literary history* considers the fool in relation to tradition.

The famous essay 'How many children had Lady Macbeth' which attacked the attitude towards Shakespeare's characters of A. C. Bradley, is printed by the author, L. C. Knights, in his *Explorations*. As already indicated in this chapter, the wheel is beginning to come full circle with studies like J. I. M. Stewart's *Character and Motive in Shakespeare*, where there is a reference to "Bradley-and-water critics". This book contains essays on the characters of Macbeth and Othello and Cleopatra. John Palmer's companion volume to his *Comic Characters* is his *Political Characters of Shakespeare*, in which he says: "The astonishing veracity of Shakespeare's political characters is due, indeed, to the small interest which he took in politics as compared with the great interest which he took in human nature." The characters considered here are Brutus, Richard III, Richard II, Henry of Monmouth, both as Prince and King, and Coriolanus. L. C. Knights in his *Further Explorations* takes up this particular theme of criticism again in his essay 'The Question of Character in Shakespeare'. E. E. Stoll, whose work on Shakespeare runs to many hundreds of pages, has written some character studies of Falstaff and Shylock and an essay on 'Characterisation in Shakespeare' in his *Shakespeare Studies: historical and comparative in method.*

William Hazlitt's *The Characters of Shakespeare's Plays* has stood the test of time, 150 years of changing fashions in literary appreciation. He says Shakespeare's characters "speak like men, not like authors". Through Hazlitt the ideas of the famous German translator of Shakespeare, A. W. von Schlegel, gained currency in Britain.

Professor A. Sewell, in his *Character and Society in Shakespeare*, outlines his views on Shakespeare's handling of character problems and then examines the implications, treating separately the comedies, histories, tragedies, and romances. He wants to take issue with J. I. M. Stewart, whose book *Character and Motive in Shakespeare* applies psychological knowledge to the study of these matters. He writes "a man writes plays partly at least because he is beset by unexpressed selves". Sewell says: "We can only understand Shakespeare's characters so long as we agree that we cannot know all about them and are not supposed to know all about them." An altogether more solid work is L. L. Schücking's *Character Problems in Shakespeare's Plays* which he sub-titles "a guide to the better understanding of the dramatist". This comprehensive analysis is arranged under headings such as 'Character and expression', 'Character and action', with the argument illustrated by references from the plays.

8. *Tales from Shakespeare's Plays*

The famous *Tales from Shakespeare* by Charles and Mary Lamb are available in several editions, the one that I prefer being that illustrated by Arthur Rackham. A number of modern authors have written their own version of the stories of Shakespeare's plays, mainly for children. The best of these is a 2-volume work of Roger Lancelyn Green, entitled *Tales from Shakespeare*; vol. 1 is confined to the comedies, and vol. 2 to the tragedies and romances. Christopher Fry has written an appreciative foreword in which he says that the Lambs miss out many of the minor characters, but that R. L. Green has them "to the life". There are some illustrations by Richard Beer. Dr. G. B. Harrison has also tried his hand at this task in his *New Tales from Shakespeare* in 2 volumes, with coloured plates by C. Walter Hodges. One of the biggest problems for a writer of tales from Shakespeare is to decide how far to let the incomparable language of the plays be lost altogether. Most of the authors make their own paraphrases for the passages of dialogue. Ian Serraillier is a popular writer of children's stories and he has made short stories of eleven of the plays which are published in an attractive little volume entitled *The Enchanted Island*. Available in paperback is *Stories from Shakespeare* by Marchette Chute. The plays are all summarized, with the exception of *Pericles*, in short chapters which outline the stories. The book has an index of characters. This book would be suitable for students wanting a quick look at all the plays and their subject-matter. Also suitable for older readers is A. J. Smith's *Shakespeare Stories*, which tells the plots of six of the plays, *Hamlet, Julius Caesar, Macbeth, Romeo and Juliet, Richard II*, and *King Lear*.

CHAPTER 7

Special Themes and Subjects

THE works of Shakespeare are a wonderful quarry for researchers who wish to probe his views. In this chapter I have grouped a few of the books which have resulted from such research under certain subject headings.

Shakespeare and Religion

Until quite recently it was usual under this heading to find authors debating whether Shakespeare was a Protestant or a Catholic, but it is more usual nowadays to find discussion on whether he was even a Christian. Roland Mushat Frye's *Shakespeare and Christian Doctrine* is a formidable treatise because the author is trained both in theology and literature; his book is divided into three parts. The first, entitled 'Critical Analyses', deals with the theological interpretations and the secular interpretations, suggesting that both are in error where they are extreme. The second part is a historical background, describing the Reformation theology and ethics. Then, under short sections such as 'Death', 'Devil', 'Election', 'Mercy', 'Repentance', and so on, he quotes from Shakespeare, equating passages from the works with the ideas of the theologians. There is an interesting appendix on 'The Roman Catholic censorship of Shakespeare: 1641–1651' in which the author examines a Second Folio copy of the Works censored under the authority of the Inquisition by an English Jesuit. John Henry de Groot's *The Shakespeares and 'The Old Faith'* is a learnedly argued attempt to present the Shakespeare

94

family as Catholic. Christopher Devlin, S.J., in a book of elegantly written essays, entitled *Hamlet's Divinity*, argues very cogently in one of them, 'Shakespeare's faith', that Shakespeare was of the Old Religion. Another writer who has written a life of Shakespeare in an attempt to present him as a Catholic is the Countess of Chambrun. While preparing material for her book, which is called *Shakespeare: a portrait restored* she turned over all kinds of documents neglected or discarded by other writers. Heinrich Mutchmann and Karl Wentersdorf have contributed a study entitled *Shakespeare and Catholicism*. The religious training that Shakespeare most likely received is the subject of T. W. Baldwin's *William Shakespeare's Petty School*, a book of 200 large, finely printed pages, describing in detail, thanks to the author's deep and prolonged study of Elizabethan education, the religious formation of children of those days. Another, less scholarly work, is by H. S. Bowden (of the London Oratory), entitled *The Religion of Shakespeare*, in which the author acknowledges his debt to the writings of Mr. Richard Simpson. A book by T. Carter, long out of print, entitled *Shakespeare: puritan and recusant*, takes the view of E. C. Fripp that John Shakespeare, the poet's father, was in trouble because of his puritanism. Canon C. Looten, of Lille, has written *Shakespeare et la religion*, of which I have not been able to trace an English translation. It discusses the treatment of religion and religious questions in the plays, and reaches some conclusions about Shakespeare's personal religion as well as outlining the religious atmosphere in London in the late sixteenth century. The author wisely comments "les matières morales ne sont pas susceptibles d'une rigueur mathématique".

Two recent essays are of great interest. Irving Ribner, in 'Shakespeare's Christianity and the Problem of Belief', *Centennial Review*, VII, 1963, asks the question "Does one's belief help one's aesthetic experience of the plays?", and Virgil K. Whitaker takes the view that Shakespeare was "intellectually a Christian" in *The Mirror Up to Nature: the technique of Shakespeare's tragedies*.

Law

G. W. Keeton, an acknowledged authority on the law of equity, in his *Shakespeare and His Legal Problems* takes themes like 'Common law and Shylock', 'International law and Shakespeare', and develops them, closely following the text and argument of the plays. He also writes critical accounts of the great trial scenes from the plays and has a chapter on the divorce of Queen Katharine in *Henry VIII*. He has followed this book up recently with a much more comprehensive work entitled *Shakespeare's Legal and Political Background*.

War

Paul A. Jorgenson, in a handsomely printed book entitled *Shakespeare's Military World*, gives the world the fruit of his researches into the extent of Shakespeare's knowledge of the ways of the military of his time. The author is Bibliographer of the Shakespeare Association of America and an associate Professor of English at University of California at Los Angeles. One of his amusing asides is that he has found no mention of the rank of sergeant in the plays. He takes all the historically important military themes, such as conscription in Elizabethan England, the Essex rebellion, the effort of officers from the disbanded armies to become peace-time courtiers, and so on, and traces the echoes of these contemporary events in the plays.

Maritime Life

A. F. Falconer, whose glossary has already been mentioned, has also compiled a little book on *Shakespeare and the Sea*. He divides his book into chapters for such nautical subjects as 'Tides', 'Pirates', 'Shipwreck', and 'Types of ship'. By quoting relevant passages from the plays he is able to show in his commentary that Shakespeare used the language of sailors accurately and was well versed in naval customs.

Nature

Sir Archibald Geikie's *The Birds of Shakespeare* is illustrated with full-page plates in black and white of the birds described in the plays. Geikie exclaimed: "Shakespeare has drawn an assemblage of bird portraits to which, for extent and variety, no equal is to be found in any other great English poet." He allots a chapter to each bird, from the eagle to the chough, and pays tribute to an earlier—Victorian—work in the subject, James Harting's *Ornithology of Shakespeare*. That Harting did his job with exceeding Victorian thoroughness is testified by the very recent handsome photolithographed reprint which has restored this book to currency. It is now entitled *The Birds of Shakespeare* with a sub-title "or an ornithology of Shakespeare critically examined, explained and illustrated". It consists of a table of ornithological allusions in the order in which they occur in the plays, these being taken in alphabetical order. The modern reprint is enriched by an essay entitled 'Of men and birds: prolegomena to the birds of Shakespeare' by Grundy Steiner.

Two other works in this field which are recommended are Lavonia Stockelback's *The Birds of Shakespeare* and Persis Kirmse's *Shakespeare and the Birds*, which is notable for its drawings.

At least one of the giants of literary criticism, Professor G. Wilson Knight, has turned his attention to this subject, and his essay on 'The Shakespeare aviary' may be found in his book *The Shakespearean Tempest*.

Medicine

R. R. Simpson's *Shakespeare and Medicine* sketches the state of medicine in sixteenth-century England, and has an interesting chapter on the influence of Shakespeare of his son-in-law, Mr. John Hall, physician. The book follows the style of other books on special subjects by taking certain themes such as 'pregnancy', 'wounds', 'drugs and poisons', and so on, and grouping illustrative quotations from the plays under these heads with a commentary.

Music

H. Kersey White compiled an invaluable *Index to the Songs, Snatches and Passages in Shakespeare which have been set to Music*, but this was in 1900. As all the world knows, Shakespeare's plays are full of musical allusions and abound in unforgettably lovely songs. Useful essays on Shakespeare and music are to be found in *Shakespeare Survey 11* and *Shakespeare Survey 15*, while in the fourth volume of the *New Oxford History of Music*, a work of majestic but flowing scholarship, a section will be found on the subject. There is a book by R. Noble entitled *Shakespeare's Use of Song*. A list of the songs that are held to be almost certainly by Shakespeare is given in F. E. Halliday's *Shakespeare Companion*. There are surprisingly only twenty-three of them. Phyllis Hartnoll edited in 1964 *Shakespeare in Music: essays, with a catalogue of musical works*, which supplements Kersey White's index. Two other books must be mentioned, both recommended by Halliday, E. W. Naylor's *Shakespeare and Music* and J. H. Long's *Shakespeare's Use of Music*.

The Shakespeare Industry

A number of very entertaining books have traced the history of Shakespeare appreciation through the centuries. Ivor Brown and George Fearon were first in the field with their *Amazing Monument: a short history of the Shakespeare industry*, which is both revealing and entertaining as well as providing an insight into the power of a great artist to move men long after his death. A similar theme preoccupies F. E. Halliday in his *The Cult of Shakespeare*, but perhaps the most thorough and entertaining of all these books is Louis Marder's *His Exits and His Entrances*, which he sub-titled "The story of Shakespeare's reputation". Although I find some of the theatrical history tedious—I would like to know so much more about the way the film industry tackles Shakespeare—the book is thoroughly entertaining from William Prynne's complaint that "Schackspere's plaies are printed on the best crowne paper, far better than most Bibles", to the report of the Zurich Drama Festival of June 1953 when a French version of *The Taming of the Shrew* was concluded by no fewer than fourteen curtain calls and "loud cries of 'Vive la France', 'Vive Shakespeare' ", which must have made Voltaire wince in his grave.

However, there is much sound scholarship in this book, which has, for instance, a chapter entitled 'Un-willingly to School'. This outlines the growth of Shakespeare studies in school, quoting Ivor Brown's lament on his own schoolday studies of Shakespeare, which left him "sickened of Shakespeare by education" and "allergic almost beyond hope of therapy" at the age of 18. He at least recovered and found his therapist. There is another fascinating chapter on 'The quest for an image' which tries to estimate the authenticity of the various portraits that purport to be of Shakespeare. He shrewdly says of the "plethora of portraits" that "God gave Shakespeare one face and his idolaters have kept fashioning others". It is in Louis Marder's pages that one comes across reference to notable forgeries, like those committed by John Payne Collier and William Henry Ireland. The latter's escapades have been recounted in a very entertaining book by Bernard Grebanier entitled *The Great Shakespeare Forgery: a new look at the career of William Henry Ireland*. The inventiveness and bulk of the forgeries, which included annotated books from Shakespeare's library, letters between the poet and Southampton, a letter from Queen Elizabeth, and even a complete missing play, *Vortigern*, which was performed at Drury Lane in 1796 with Kemble in the lead. This William Henry told his own story in his *Confessions*. If you want to know whether he was exposed in his lifetime, you must read either these or Bernard Grebanier's book. Suffice to say that William Henry's father Samuel was also a very tricky character, and be careful not to confuse the two. A shorter account of the pair of them is to be found both in Louis Marder and in F. E. Halliday's *Cult of Shakespeare*.

Another aspect of Shakespeare history that is dealt with in these books is the famous Shakespeare jubilee arranged and presided over by David Garrick in 1769. Carola Oman has written a life, *David Garrick*, which fits this episode into the rest of his career. Two books at least have been written by authors who have gone to some pains to tell the whole story in detail. These are *The Great Shakespeare Jubilee* by Christian Deelman which is "an account of David Garrick's worship of Shakespeare and of the first Shakespeare festival organised by him in 1769 at Stratford", and *Garrick's Folly: the Stratford Jubilee of 1769*, which is by Johanne M. Stochholm.

Shakespeare in Russia

The popularity of Shakespeare in Russia has survived the imposition of the Soviet system and in *Shakespeare in the Soviet Union*, published in Moscow, a collection of articles by Russian authors has been collected by the Commission for the Study of Shakespeare which is a body attached to the Institute of World Literature of the U.S.S.R. Academy of Sciences. Part I contains articles on Shakespeare and the study of literature, on Alexander Blok, the revolutionary poet, and on *King Lear*. Part II is on *Shakespeare and the Theatre*, and has an article by Ulanova on 'My Juliet'.

CHAPTER 8

The Sonnets and Poems

LAWRENCE DURRELL has described the mysteries of Shakespeare's sonnets as the source of one of the most enjoyable of literary pastimes—who was the young Friend of the first 126 sonnets? Who is the Dark Lady with the loose morals—was she a Negress, a notorious harlot, or a lady-in-waiting of Queen Elizabeth's strictly controlled court where adultery was so frowned on that even so considerable a magnate as Southampton was imprisoned and disgraced for refusing to marry a lady he had got with child? Who was the rival poet whom Shakespeare envied? G. Wilson Knight, in his *The Mutual Flame: on Shakespeare's Sonnets and The Phoenix and the Turtle*, puts the problem succinctly: "We do not know when they were written, to whom they were addressed, nor even if they are certainly autobiographical." C. S. Lewis, in his well-known and much-praised *English Literature in the Sixteenth Century* (which it must be remembered excludes the drama from its scope), says that when the sonnet sequence is read through at a sitting "from its total plot, however ambiguous, however particular, there emerges something not indeed common or general like the love expressed in many individual sonnets, but yet, in a higher way, universal". He goes on to claim that the sonnets open a new world of love poetry, and it is to the sonnet which contrasts the two loves, that of 'comfort' and that of 'despair' that one should turn first.

> Two loves I have of comfort and despair,
> Which like two spirits do suggest me still,
> The better angel is a man right fair:
> The worser spirit a woman coloured ill.
> To win me soon to hell my female evil,

> Tempteth my better angel from my side,
> And would corrupt my saint to be a devil:
> Wooing his purity with her foul pride.
> And whether that my angel be turned fiend,
> Suspect I may, yet not directly tell,
> But being both from me both to each friend,
> I guess one angel in another's hell.
>> Yet this shall I ne'er know but live in doubt,
>> Till my bad angel fire my good one out.

Is this a philosophical poem, or does Shakespeare mean that he suspects his "better angel" has taken the "woman coloured ill" for a mistress, and she's a whore, he'll not know unless he contracts venereal disease from her? The bewilderment the sonnets have caused is admirably summed up in the exclamations of Leon de Wailly who said in 1834: "Good heavens! . . . He instead of she? Can I be mistaken? Can these sonnets be addressed to a man? Shakespeare! Great Shakespeare!"

Then there is the mystery of the 1609 Quarto edition; why have so few copies survived? Only thirteen against several hundred First Folios? Was the edition withdrawn from circulation? Shakespeare was always a popular poet whose works sold well. Then why was it that no fresh edition appeared until 1639 and that a pirated edition by a certain John Benson, who changed the "he's" to "she's" in the opening sequence, and ran sonnets together to form longer poems which he gave fanciful titles? Is the order of the sonnets in the 1609 Quarto the order Shakespeare wished, and chose himself? When were the sonnets written? We know that the sonnet on the two loves quoted above and one other were printed in a collection of poems entitled *The Passionate Pilgrim* which was published in 1599, and the two sonnets are number 138 and 144 in the sequence. Had all the others already been written? It is held that only one of the sonnets has any material that could be dated from contemporary events, namely the 107th:

> The mortal moon hath her eclipse endured,
> And the sad augurs mock their own presage,
> Incertainties now crown themselves assured,
> And peace proclaims olives of endless age.

Is the "mortal moon" Queen Elizabeth, in which case what "eclipse" had she "endured"—or is it a reference to the crescent shape of the Spanish fleet as the invasion Armada sailed into the Channel? According to the years in which it is held the sonnets were written, so can the identification of the characters of the poems proceed. There is endless opportunity for speculation here.

There is the question of the dedication. Who was the "Mr. W. H." whom the publisher Thomas Thorpe claims as the "onlie begetter" of the sonnets? Does it mean William Himself, or is it a reference to William Herbert, the Earl of Pembroke, or some one else? Then there is the question of the poem *Willobie His Avisa* in which there is a section telling how a certain "W. S." had a passion for Avisa and is asked to advise his friend H. W. who has a like affliction. Is this "W. S." William Shakespeare and is there any connection between Avisa and the Dark Lady? It seems very unlikely if one reads the bawdy sonnets 135 and 136.

However, fortunately it is not my job to unravel the mysteries of the sonnets, and, as Lawrence Durrell says, it would be a pity if anyone did, but only to draw attention to some of the books on the subject.

To start with editions: there are two which recommend themselves to the untried reader by their simplicity. One is the Penguin edition edited by G. B. Harrison, which prints the sonnets two to a page in the order of the 1609 Quarto, with modernized spelling and typography, but with only minor changes to the punctuation which Harrison calls "subtle and striking". This edition also has the merit of reprinting the poem *A Lover's Complaint*, which was part of the 1609 Quarto but has been ignored since then. Its subject-matter, the lament of a young girl over a beautiful young man who has betrayed her, has obvious reference to the theme of some of the sonnets.

C. S. Lewis has written it off as "poetically inconsiderable" and "unlike Shakespeare". Dr. Harrison lists eleven problems raised by the sonnets, but he wisely refrains from trying to solve them. His notes are more in the nature of a simple glossary. This is a pleasant edition to handle and easy to carry in one's pocket.

The other edition, although published very recently, has already been much commended: *Shakespeare's Sonnets*, edited with an introduction and notes by Martin Seymour-Smith. It is a reprint of the text of the 1609 Quarto, retaining the original spelling and punctuation with very few slight changes, all of which are noted in the text. The introduction briefly sets out the problems that the sonnets present with an equally brief consideration of the solutions proposed. It is a masterpiece of scholarly compression, and the arguments are so tightly organized that it is difficult to see how the task could be done better. The commentary which follows the text is fairly extensive, and a very cogent and consistent argument is built up, sonnet by sonnet, to sustain the editor's own views on the answer to the mysteries that have baffled the reader for so long. The edition of the *Sonnets* which everyone praises is that of *The New Variorium Shakespeare* in 2 volumes, edited by E. Rollins and published in Philadelphia in 1944. Its notes comprise those of all previous editors and outline and sum up all the various arguments of the commentators. Behind all the editors stands the figure of Edmond Malone, whose edition of the *Sonnets* was published in 1780, and Mr. Seymour-Smith has a paragraph which admirably explains all that subsequent editors owe to Malone as well as the reasons why he is not an altogether satisfactory editor.

> His was the first scholarly edition, and his annotations are still valuable. Unfortunately, however, Malone edited, emended and modernised according to the standards of poetic diction prevalent in his own not very critically enlightened times. The result is not altogether Shakespeare. Malone's re-punctuation, followed more or less by all modernizing editors, ignores both poetic subtlety and rhythmic function. The distortion of meaning is never great, but the elimination of difficulties and ambiguities that are an inherent part of the text results in impoverishment of the poetry.

This view is supported by Laura Riding and Robert Graves, who many years before Seymour-Smith's edition of the *Sonnets*, had written in their *A Survey of Modern Poetry* that the text of 1609 edition of the *Sonnets* reproduced down to the smallest detail what Shakespeare had actually written. They rejected all the emendations made by later editors, saying that these "simplified

Shakespeare" and "only weakened and diluted his poetry".
L. C. Knights approved this opinion in his essay on 'Shakespeare's
Sonnets' in *Scrutiny* III, 1934.

The most recent edition of the Sonnets is the final volume in the
New Cambridge Shakespeare, whose veteran editor, John Dover
Wilson, went blind while at work on it. At the same time, A. L.
Rowse was preparing his edition of the *Sonnets*, Dover Wilson
amusingly describes the advance publication of his draft introduction while newspaper readers were getting the views of A. L.
Rowse in a series of articles: "thus it came about that when his
Cornish privateer of tall building and of goodly pride put forth
into the perilous main of publicity, full of 'literary' submarines,
my saucy bark, dressed overall in Cambridge blue and with
pennon flying inscribed *For historians and others*, was there riding
alongside." Dover Wilson accepts Seymour-Smith's view that the
punctuation of the Quarto text must be left virtually as it is. Although he follows most of the "modernizations" of Malone's text
which Seymour-Smith deplores, he regrets the fact, saying that
"modernization is attended with almost as many risks as emendation". The long introduction to this edition, over 100 pages of it, is
divided into sections: 'The origin and quality of the received text';
'The Friend and the Poet'; 'The identity of Mr. W. H.'; 'Themes
and sources', which argue a solution to all the familiar problems.
The notes at the end of the book are equally extensive.

Shakespeare's Sonnets, edited with an introduction and notes by
A. L. Rowse, is a large, handsome volume, as Dover Wilson infers.
The sonnets are printed one to a page on the left-hand pages with
a prose paraphrase which sticks fairly closely, however, to the
phraseology of the sonnets, on the right-hand page, followed, in
smaller print, by a commentary, in which the author reasons out
his answers to the various problems. Rowse's short introduction,
in which he attempts to date the sonnets and identify the persons
to whom they were addressed, is particularly interesting because
of his profound and detailed knowledge of the period and his
historian's awareness that "one should not be so blithe with the
years, that there is all the difference in the world even between one

year and the next". He, too, is satisfied that "the Sonnets, as we have them, tell an intelligible story, and any attempt to rearrange them is otiose and absurd".

Leslie Hotson is an indefatigable searcher through Elizabethan documents in the Public Record Office. In his book *Mr. W. H.* he makes a deep ranging survey of Elizabethan literature, following up clues of all kinds from one book to another, checking facts and details in the archives; employing methods which he describes as "something more like the routine work of the Criminal Investigation Department at New Scotland Yard". Moreover, he claims to have run the man whom George Sampson called "that embarrassing phantom" to earth and identified him. Whatever the scholars may think of the answer, no one will deny that the investigation is very enjoyable.

The rival poet, who is addressed so directly in Sonnet 86, is thought by most writers to have been George Chapman, the famous translator of Homer, but Robert Gittings, in his *Shakespeare's Rival*, suggests that it was a minor poet named Gervase Markham, which idea has not won much favour. Oscar Wilde's piece *Portrait of Mr. W. H.* is scarcely more than an agreeable fiction. *Willobie His Avisa* was reprinted by G. B. Harrison whose explanation of the problems raised by the poem has won a wide measure of acceptance.

Two books of literary and philosophical criticism are J. B. Leishman's *Themes and Variations in Shakespeare's Sonnets*, a book of which Professor Dover Wilson thinks highly; and G. Wilson Knight's *The Mutual Flame* in which there is a fascinating chapter entitled 'Time and eternity'. "Poetic insight", says Knight, "is made from various stabs of insight" and one feels that the critic here has had a stab of insight which has only been partially developed, for there seems to be very much more to be said on this idea that one of the themes of the sonnets is Shakespeare's "attack on Time". A. C. Bradley, of course, in his *Oxford Lectures on Poetry*, has valuable things to say about the sonnets, as has J. W. Lever in his often-quoted *The Elizabethan Love Sonnet*.

A useful short account of Shakespeare's sonnets and poems is to be found in the British Council pamphlet written by F. T. Prince and entitled *William Shakespeare: the poems*. Published in 1963 the pamphlet has a bibliography valuable for its noting of papers available in a number of British and North American journals.

Studies of the poetry of Shakespeare's plays as distinct from the poetry's part in the dramas, are also numerous. M. C. Bradbrook, in her *Shakespeare and Elizabethan Poetry*, subtitled "a study of his earlier work in relation to the poetry of his time", has attempted something which she herself admits is a mighty task. As her book is read and studied with gratitude she must have had a measure of success in achieving what is indicated in her sub-title. A book which traces the progress of Shakespeare's verse from the early years of apprenticeship to the later ones of complete mastery is F. E. Halliday's *The Poetry of Shakespeare's Plays*.

> The author states: there is no one Shakespearean style, no one Shakespearean poetry, but at least five, corresponding roughly to the five periods which he sets out as 1. The early histories and comedies, 1590–94; 2. Lyrical plays 1594–97; 3. Histories and romantic comedies 1597–1601; 4. Tragedies 1601–08; 5. Romances 1608–13.

Lord Ivor Evans, in his *The Language of Shakespeare's Plays*, wishes to counteract some of the excesses of the Spurgeon school of critics; he writes:

> I have emphasised that imagery . . . is only one part of Shakespeare's language. I have followed through the plays, commenting on the problems that faced Shakespeare . . . he was always in a sort of splendid peril . . . of being overwhelmed by the exuberance of his own verbal genius. . . . I have tried to emphasise . . . that language in drama must be referred to the effect which it can make in the theatre.

The last sentence marks this as a recent study, insisting on a now familiar theme. Professor Evans reminds his readers that "much that was most moving in his plays was written in the simplest language without any dependence on those great sources of imagery which he had always at his command".

Closer studies of the use of words in Shakespeare is to be found in Professor Empson's *Structure of Complex Words*, in which he has chapters on the use of the word "Fool" in *Lear*; of the word "sense" in *Measure for Measure*; the word "honest" in *Othello*, and the word "dog" in *Timon of Athens*. He says in the latter chapter: "I shall try to show that Shakespeare is both presenting and refusing a set of feelings about *dog* as metaphor, making it in effect a term of praise." Maud Bodkin, in her *Archetypal Patterns in Poetry*, also a very famous book, has studies of the poetry of *Hamlet*, *Othello*, and *Lear*; her interpretation is, of course, psychology based.

Finally, M. M. Mahood's study of the dramatic function of the pun in *Shakespeare's Wordplay*, with particular reference to its use in *Romeo and Juliet*, *Richard II*, *Hamlet*, *Macbeth*, and *The Winter's Tale*, must not be omitted.

A very full bibliography of works on English poetry in the sixteenth century with a section on Shakespeare's sonnets and poems is included in Professor C. S. Lewis's *English Literature in the Sixteenth Century, Excluding Drama*.

CHAPTER 9

Commentaries on Individual Plays

G. H. HARDY writes in his book *A Mathematician's Apology* that "Exposition, criticism, appreciation, is work for second-rate minds". It is just as well before embarking on a survey of the criticism of Shakespeare's plays to realize what a pygmy Shakespeare makes of the greatest of scholars. Very little that has been written about him approaches in quality even the meanest work that he wrote himself. However, although this must be said, it must also be said that the scholars are today in a fair way to rescuing the work of Shakespeare from what he most feared, namely misrepresentation; better, I feel, Shakespeare would have said, oblivion than that. The scholars, by their patient remorseless unravellings have uncovered so much of the truth of the late sixteenth and early seventeenth centuries that we of this age can almost claim contemporaneity with Shakespeare, and thus his plays can be presented today with more understanding than at any time since he himself was responsible for their production.

Some half-hours spent with the relevant pages of the *Year's Work in English Studies* and the review of the year's work in *Shakespeare Survey* plus the abstracts printed in the Cincinnati *Shakespeare Studies* will reveal to the inquiring student more riches of research than he had dreamed of.

Some of the *Elizabethan Bibliographies* published in New York since the war pertain to one of Shakespeare's plays, and contain upward of 2000 items each. Judge, then, the task of the student who is to read just a few essays. What a colossal sea of criticism must for ever be unknown to him, as to everyone else. No one man can surely at this date read everything, or even a fraction of everything that has been written about Shakespeare. The trouble with the *Elizabethan Bibliographies* is that they make no attempt to discriminate between the items they list.

What follows in this chapter is a discursive account of some of the work on the individual plays which happens to interest the present writer; it is presented as an example of what can be discovered using the bibliographical aids mentioned above. Certain plays and problems have a fascination for me which I fear I shall betray by lingering over references to works about them. I take the plays in alphabetical order.

All's Well That Ends Well

Osbert Lancaster, in his introduction to the Folio Society edition of the play, finds little to recommend it apart from "the contrast of the two main settings. On the one hand Rossillion and the Court of France, medieval, old-fashioned, hierarchic; on the other, Renaissance Florence, tough, realistic, modern."

Antony and Cleopatra

The contrast of Rome's order and morality with Egypt's wit, youthful high spirits, and genius for fun is the theme of many studies, such as John F. Danby's 'The Shakespearean dialectic: an aspect of *Antony and Cleopatra*', in *Scrutiny*, XVI (1949), and Eugene M. Waith's 'Manhood and valor in two Shakespearean tragedies', in *ELH*, XVII (1950). "The quality of experience to be met with in the respective characters' stage lives rather than in the ideas implicit in them" is considered in A. Caputi's 'Shakespeare's *Antony and Cleopatra*: tragedy without terror', in *Shakespeare Quarterly*, XVI (1965). In his anthology of modern criticism, *Shakespeare's Tragedies*, Laurence Lerner choses for his section on *Antony and Cleopatra* a portion of Granville-Barker's *Preface*, on the construction of the play, and a few pages from J. Middleton Murry's *Problem of Style*, instancing the scene in which Cleopatra dies as the "absolute perfection" of style. Murry warns that "only when you have truly apprehended a work of literature are you in a position to make positive declarations about its style". Lerner also prints an essay by W. K. Wimsatt from his the *Verbal Icon*, on the morality of the play. Wimsatt reminds the reader that: "What is celebrated in *Antony and Cleopatra* is the passionate surrender to an illicit love, the victory of this love over practical, political, and moral concerns, and the final superiority of the suicide lovers over circumstance." Indeed, "a crudely one-sided statement which makes the play as plainly immoral as it can be made".

As You Like It

C. L. Barber, in his chapter on *As You Like It* in his *Shakespeare's Festive Comedy*, quotes T. S. Eliot's comment on Marvell and the metaphysical poets as showing "an alliance of levity and seriousness (by which the seriousness is intensified)". He develops this theme in his study of the play, quoting T. S. Eliot again to remind his readers that the play contains some of the greatest prose in our language. S. L. Bethell, in his *Shakespeare and the Popular Dramatic Tradition*, has a short section on Touchstone. The theme of time is considered by Jay L. Halio in his 'No cloak in the forest', in *Studies in English Literature*, II (1962). The contrasts so beloved of Shakespeare are present numerously in this play, as Harold Jenkins makes plain in his '*As You Like It*' essay in *Shakespeare Survey 8*.

Comedy of Errors

Derek Traversi's *Shakespeare: the early comedies* includes an account of the play. G. R. Elliott's 'Weirdness in the *Comedy of Errors*', appeared in *University of Toronto Quarterly*, 1939, and is reprinted in Laurence Lerner's *Shakespeare's Comedies*.

Coriolanus

In his introductory essay to his edition of *Coriolanus* in the *New Penguin Shakespeare*, G. R. Hibbard refutes the arguments that this is a bleak play and says it is "an affirmation of the values of honesty, kindness and relationship, and of the fundamental importance of 'the human heart by which we live'." Hibbard gives a good account of criticism of the play, noting A. C. Bradley's British Academy Lecture published in *A Miscellany*, 1929, and G. Wilson Knight's treatment of the play in *The Imperial Theme*, 1931, as presenting different views of the play's success. L. C. Knights, in *Some Shakespearean Themes*, 1959, and *Further Explorations*, 1965, writes of the political wisdom of the play, a view supported by F. N. Lees in his article '*Coriolanus*, Aristotle and Bacon' which appeared in the *Review of English Studies*, 1950. Hibbard also commends Maurice Charney's *Shakespeare's Roman Plays*, 1961, as "the most thorough analysis of the imagery that has yet been made". In *Papers Mainly Shakespearean*, edited by G. I. Duthie, D. J. Gordon has an essay 'Name and fame: Shakespeare's *Coriolanus*', analysing the key concepts of "honour", "voice", "name", "rumour", and "fame" in terms of classical and Renaissance ideas.

Cymbeline

There is an essay by A. A. Stephenson called 'The significance of *Cymbeline*', *Scrutiny*, X, 1942. Bernard Shaw wrote an entire new fifth act to the play in 1937, his only attempt at blank verse. There is a good short account of the play in D. A. Traversi's *Shakespeare: the last phase*, in which it is pointed out that *Cymbeline*, like *Pericles*, was an experimental play, leading to the "finished achievement" of *The Winter's Tale*.

Hamlet

Paul S. Conklin has written *A History of Hamlet Criticism: 1601–1821* which is an admirable account of the opinions expressed during that period. A. J. A. Waldock's *Hamlet: a study in critical method*, 1931, provides a guide to *Hamlet* criticism as far as Bradley. M. R. Ridley, in his edition of the play, says of Bradley's essay in his famous *Shakespearean Tragedy* on *Hamlet* that "Even where all is excellent the section on *Hamlet* stands out, because of the balance which the critic manages to maintain in executing a task of peculiar difficulty. He is conducting a subtle and penetrating analysis of character; and yet he never forgets that the character he is analysing is a character in a play." The book of J. Dover Wilson's *What Happens in Hamlet* considers what the Elizabethan audience would have made of the play. This book has a high reputation. All the famous critics have tried their hand at interpreting *Hamlet* and trying to solve the mystery of his procrastination. I like the critic who said that Shakespeare had five acts to write, that is why Hamlet delayed. G. Wilson Knight, in 'The embassy of death' contained in his *The Wheel of Fire*, makes Hamlet some sort of villain of the piece; William Empson, in 'Hamlet when new' published in *Sewanee Review*, 1933, writes of *Hamlet* as a revenge play. A Spanish critic of considerable reputation, Salvador de Madariaga, devoted a whole book *On Hamlet* to the presentation of a foreigner's view of England's most famous tragedy. L. Forest, in *PMLA* LXI (1946), has an essay 'A caveat for critics against invoking Elizabethan psychology'. C. S. Lewis, in his British Academy Lecture 'Hamlet: the prince or the poem', reprinted in Peter Alexander's *Studies in Shakespeare* begins his paper by confessing that he can make "no claim to be a true Shakespearean scholar". He says that "In a sense, the subject of *Hamlet* is death". He quotes with approval T. S. Eliot's comment that "more people have thought *Hamlet* a work of art because they found it interesting, than have found it interesting because it is a work of art". Another much-praised study is in D. G. James's *The Dream of Learning*, in which *Hamlet* is discussed along with *King Lear*, and Bacon's *Advancement of Learning*. Maynard Mack's 'The world of Hamlet', which appeared in the *Yale Review*, 1952, and has been reprinted in Cleanth Brooks's *Tragic Themes in Western Literature*, is also often quoted. *Shakespeare Survey 9* has a number of articles devoted to the study of *Hamlet*. L. C. Knights's *An Approach to Hamlet* has some subtle remarks to make about Shakespeare's preoccupation with man's subjection to illusion—"the seeming truth which cunning times put on to entrap the wisest". J. I. M. Stewart, under his pen-name as a detective story writer, Michael Innes, collaborated with Rayner Heppenstall in an entertaining book *Three Tales of Hamlet*. A. S. Cairncross has boldly written *The Problem of Hamlet: a solution*, though perhaps without the confidence of Ernest Jones whose study of *Hamlet*, first published in the *American Journal of Psychology*, 1910, was published in book form in 1949 as *Hamlet and Oedipus*, a study of Hamlet's "tortured conscience". It is a hopeless task to make a selection from all the absorbing literature on Hamlet. I shall conclude this section with a mention of a study that interests me very much: 'Shakespeare's anti-hero: Hamlet and the underground man' by Stanley Cooperman, which appeared in *Shakespeare Studies*, I, 1965. The author uses the question of Dostoevsky's character: "can a man of perception respect himself at all?" to conduct an inquiry into Shakespeare's presentation of Hamlet. A useful bibliography is to be found in M. Weitz's *Hamlet and the Philosophy of Literary Criticism*.

Henry IV, Parts I and II

After Hamlet, there is probably no character who has attracted so much attention as Falstaff. Maurice Morgann's *An Essay on the Dramatic Character of Sir John Falstaff*, which first appeared in 1777, is still available. The modern critic, equipped with his reading of Frazer and Freud, goes in a different direction from Morgann, as Harold F. Toliver in 'Falstaff and the Prince and the History Play', *Shakespeare Quarterly*, XVI, 1965. Shakespeare had an extraordinary grasp of the realities of politics, and it seems to me that he handled some themes that were potentially explosive in the years in which he wrote, but he escaped any censure because he knew what he was doing. G. K. Hunter has an essay on 'Shakespeare's politics and the rejection of Falstaff' in *Critical Quarterly*, I, 1959, and W. H. Auden's 'The fallen city: some reflections on Shakespeare's *Henry IV*' which appeared in *Encounter*, XIII, 1959, is of great interest in this connection. Ronald Berman is concerned with 'The nature of guilt in the Henry IV plays', *Shakespeare Studies*, I, 1965, in which he writes about "the language of inhumanity" in the plays. J. D. Wilson has written in his usual absorbing way of *The Fortunes of Falstaff*.

Another fascinating study is Robert Hapgood's 'Falstaff's vocation', because he will have none of Dover Wilson's attempt to clear Falstaff's reputation of crime. Hapgood, whose paper appeared in *Shakespeare Quarterly*, XVI, 1965, begins with the words: "So robber robs robber in an endless circle", and portrays Falstaff as a thief, saying that stealing was not merely his vocation, but "is integral to his character, and a key to it". William Empson, in his 'Falstaff and Mr. Dover Wilson', which appeared in *Kenyon Review*, 1953, considers that Shakespeare was at least ambiguous about Falstaff's criminality. H. C. Goddard, in his *The Meaning of Shakespeare*, expresses extreme views and looks upon the young Prince Hal as a man trying, vainly perhaps, to escape from the encircling thefts: "It makes a difference whether you steal retail or wholesale", says the ironic Mr. Goddard.

Henry V

A great work of criticism on the 'Age of kings' plays is plainly in the making, but has not yet, I fancy, appeared. D. A. Traversi's *Shakespeare from Richard II to Henry V* is a foretaste of what will come. Joan Webber's essay 'The renewal of the king's symbolic role: from *Richard II* to *Henry V*', *Texas Studies in Language and Literature*, 1962, is another "throw-forward". There is also something good in P. Jorgensen's *Shakespeare's Military World*, and the historian M. M. Reese's *The Cease of Majesty*.

Henry VI, Parts I, II, and III

L. G. Salingar, in his essay 'The Elizabethan literary renaissance' (in Boris Ford's collection *The Age of Shakespeare*) writes: "In shaping, compressing, and altering the chronicles, Shakespeare gained the art of dramatic design; and in the same way he developed his remarkable insight into character, its continuity and its variation." I think Shakespeare also had extraordinary insight into the nature of kingship, a theme which still awaits close and historically informed study, for it is a realm somewhat removed from the more usual concerns of the literary critic and expositor.

Henry VIII

In his *Crown of Life* G. Wilson Knight argues that this play is Shakespeare's unaided work, denying Fletcher's co-authorship which is assumed by such critics as C. Leech in his *The John Fletcher Plays*. E. M. W. Tillyard contributed a paper to *Critical Quarterly*, 1961, entitled 'Why did Shakespeare write Henry VIII?'

Julius Caesar

Norman Sanders, in his introduction to his edition of this play in the *New Penguin Shakespeare*, writes that critics "have disagreed frequently in trying to define what *kind* of play it is". Professor Sanders recommends as a general study W. Warde Fowler's 'The tragic element in Shakespeare's *Julius Caesar*', published in *Transactions of the Royal Society of Literature*, XXIX, 1911. He thinks the best statements of the case against Caesar are to be found in J. Dover Wilson's preface to his Cambridge edition of the play and in Irving Ribner's 'Political issues in Julius Caesar', published in *Journal of English and Germanic Philology*, LVI, 1957. Fortunately, J. C. Maxwell in *Shakespeare Survey 10* has written a 'Survey of criticism 1900–56' and Professor Sanders's own short chapter on 'Further reading' in his New Penguin edition of the play brings this survey up to date.

King John

Was King John a villainous failure or a national hero, resisting the power of the papacy? In *Shakespeare Studies*, I, 1965, John R.

Elliott discusses the alternatives in his 'Shakespeare and the double image of King John'. By far the most detailed critical work on this play is by E. A. J. Honigmann in the introduction to his Arden edition.

King Lear

Dr. Johnson confessed that he was so shocked by Cordelia's death that, to quote his words, "I know not whether I ever endured to read again the last scenes of the play till I undertook to revise them as an editor". In recent years there have been many essays and short studies of the play, but all study, as of the other great tragedies, must begin with A. C. Bradley. Nicholas Brookes's *Shakespeare: King Lear* presents the play in all its starkness: "Large orders collapse: but values remain, and are independent of them." The theme of order is studied in Leo Kirschbaum's essay 'Albany', *Shakespeare Survey 13*, 1960, and 'The role of Albany' by Peter Mortenson, *Shakespeare Quarterly*, XVI, 1965. L. C. Knights, in the collection *The Age of Shakespeare*, edited by Boris Ford, has an essay on '*King Lear* and the great tragedies' in which he says that *Lear* is "the great central masterpiece, the great exploratory allegory, to which the earlier plays lead and on which the later tragedies depend". Knights points out in this fine study that the pessimism of the play is transcended by "the love and forgiveness of Cordelia". Granville-Barker's essay on *Lear* in his *Prefaces to Shakespeare*, First Series, is another important study, as is J. F. Danby's *Shakespeare's Doctrine of Nature: a study of King Lear*, and Theodore Spencer's *Shakespeare and the Nature of Man*, to which L. C. Knights admits a considerable debt. D. A. Traversi's essay in *Scrutiny*, XIX, 1952, entitled '*King Lear*', is also valuable. I personally can never forget Lear's Fool played by Stephen Haggard, and know of no study of that role as perceptive as Haggard's playing of it.

Love's Labour's Lost

James L. Calderwood writes in his '*Love's Labour's Lost*: a wantoning with words', published in *Studies in English Literature 1500–1900*, V, 1965, "the ideal relationship of poet and language is one of mutual enrichment—the dramatic use of language, in which words become a medium of public exchange in the theater, circulating among poets, actors and audience, and kept 'good' by the common involvement of all three in them". By any standards, *Love's Labour's Lost* is a feast of words. There are numerous articles and essays on the play, and two longer studies, E. L. Clark's *The Satirical Comedy of Love's Labour's Lost* and M. C. Bradbrook's *The School of Night*.

Macbeth

There is a vast literature on the subject of this tragedy. G. K. Hunter, in *Shakespeare Survey 19* (1966), surveys some of it in his '*Macbeth* in the twentieth century', and provides a brief summary of the major critical works through the centuries. His own study of the play appears in his *New Penguin Shakespeare* edition. J. R. Brown, in *Shakespeare: the Tragedy of Macbeth*, also includes a survey of recent studies. There are several very famous essays, such as De Quincey's 'On the knocking on the gate in *Macbeth*' and Cleanth Brooks 'The naked babe and the cloak of manliness' which appears in his book *The Well-wrought Urn*; L. C. Knights took up a theme in his 'How many children had Lady Macbeth', reprinted in his *Explorations*. Lady Macbeth is the main subject of Maynard Mack's 'The Jacobean Shakespeare' in *Jacobean Theatre*, 1960. E. M. W. Tillyard includes the play in his *Shakespeare's History Plays*; and Caroline Spurgeon devotes much space to it in her *Shakespeare's Imagery*. G. B. Harrison thought the play had many faults. A. C. Bradley gives a memorable account of the poetry's creation of the play's atmosphere of tumult and storm. G. Wilson Knight's essay 'The milk of concord', in *The Imperial Theme*, traces the life-theme and the death-theme. Kenneth Muir, in his introduction to his Arden edition, is very concerned about the Porter scene. G. I. Duthie, in *Shakespeare Survey 19* (1966), in one of his last essays, writes of 'Antithesis in *Macbeth*', and in the same issue, which has a special section on the play, W. Moelwyn Merchant writes on 'His fiend-like Queen'.

Measure for Measure

R. W. Chambers has written some of the noblest criticism in the English language. His best Shakespearean essay is, I think, '*Measure for Measure*', which is printed in *Shakespeare Criticism, 1935–1960*, edited by Ann Ridler, also known by her married name, Mrs. Bradby. He deals very effectively with hostile opinions on the play, which have the backing of Coleridge who found it distasteful. This dislike of *Measure for Measure* is almost a tradition in Shakespeare criticism, and is most rationally explained in William Empson's 'Sense in *Measure for Measure*', which is chapter 13 in his *Structure of Complex Words*. He says of the play that it "is I think one of the most striking cases where the feelings in his words jib at a wholehearted acceptance of the story, without being planned as a secret meaning for the wiser few or even marking a clear-cut opinion of the author". This is not at all the view of F. R. Leavis in his essay in *The Common Pursuit* where he castigates rival critics, notably A. C. Bradley, as suffering from "the incapacity for dealing with poetic drama, that innocence about the nature of convention and the conventional possibilities of Shakespeare's dramatic method and form. . . ." Strong words when applied to men who have devoted their lives to studying just that. Mary Lascelles, in her notable book *Shakespeare's Measure for Measure*, writes: "many objections will be found levelled against the edition of the play in the New Cambridge Shakespeare" and cautions against "any hasty interpretations of *Measure for Measure*, or any which hardens into formula", for these will "approach misconstruction". Another study which is in agreement with the Chambers' view is J. W. Bennett's *Measure for Measure as Royal Entertainment*; she treats of the play as one of forgiveness and reconciliation, and includes for her good measure, a study of Shakespeare as an actor. It is good to remember that Walter Pater, in his *Appreciations*, was most perceptively approving of the play. The theme of Christian mercy being superior to the principles of equity is discussed in John W. Dickinson's 'Renaissance equity and *Measure for Measure*', in *Shakespeare Quarterly*, XIII, 1962.

Merchant of Venice

Two recent studies of the play are W. Moelwyn Merchant's introduction to his *New Penguin Shakespeare* edition of the play and A. D. Moody's *The Merchant of Venice* in the Studies in English Literature Series edited by David Daiches. This latter is written in an engagingly trenchant style, Bassanio, for instance, being referred to as a "matinée idol". The author states his belief that "the final use of the play, as of all good art, is to make us better acquainted with the world and with ourselves". Barbara Lewalski, in her paper 'Biblical allusion and allegory in *The Merchant of Venice*', *Shakespeare Quarterly*, XIII, 1962, claims to have uncovered in the play "patterns of Biblical allusion and imagery so precise and pervasive as to be patently deliberate", and thinks it plain that Shakespeare is ultimately concerned with the nature of Christian living and love. Mr. Moody, on the other hand, gives chapter and verse for thinking that Shakespeare is taking a fair swipe at the morals of the Christian Venetians. *Early Shakespeare*, No. 3 of the Stratford-upon-Avon Studies, has an essay from Frank Kermode on 'The mature comedies' and one by J. R. Brown, who edited the 1955 Arden edition of the play, on 'The realization of Shylock'. G. Wilson Knight's *Shakespearean Production* has a great deal to say about the acting of this play. W. H. Auden's essay 'Brothers and others', in his collection *The Dyer's Hand*, and B. D. N. Grebanier's book *The Truth About Shylock*, are fascinating studies.

Merry Wives of Windsor

W. Green's *Shakespeare's Merry Wives of Windsor* is not so much about the play as about "the events surrounding its composition and the manner in which those events shaped the text of the play from its initial performance through to the 1623 Folio printing".

Midsummer Night's Dream

James L. Calderwood, in his essay '*A Midsummer Night's Dream*: the illusion of drama', which appeared in the *Modern Language Quarterly*, XXVI, 1965, says that the play should be considered as "one phase of Shakespeare's continuing exploration of the nature, value and function of art". He asks whether Shakespeare, in Bottom's words, had "a dream past the wit of man to say what dream it was" and if he had, then, again in Bottom's words, was man "an ass if he go about to expound this dream". Which comment should give the critic pause. A fascinating history of the play's presentation on the stage is provided in W. Moelwyn Merchant's '*A Midsummer Night's Dream*: a visual recreation', which appeared in *Early Shakespeare*, Stratford-upon-Avon Studies, No. 3. R. Watkins, in his *Moonlight at the Globe*, attempted "an essay in Shakespearean production based on a performance of *Midsummer Night's Dream* at Harrow School". Two papers mentioned with approval by Stanley Wells in his *New Penguin Shakespeare* edition of the play are Georges A. Bonnard's 'Shakespeare's purpose in *A Midsummer Night's Dream*', *Shakespeare Jahrbuch*, XCII, 1956, and Paul A. Olson's '*A Midsummer Night's Dream* and the meaning of court marriage', which appeared in *ELH*, XXIV, 1957. Another essay, which appeals to me, is R. W. Dent's 'Imagination in *A Midsummer Night's Dream*', *Shakespeare Quarterly*, XV, 1964, because of the summing up of the play as "a delightful exposition of the follies produced by excessive imagination in love and the pleasures produced by controlled imagination in art".

Much Ado About Nothing

"There is something pathetic", writes A. P. Rossiter in his section on this play in his *Angel with Horns*, "in the detailed scholarship which laboriously strives to conjure from its grave every ghost of an expired laugh." Nonetheless he does examine the famous wit of this play in some detail. He thinks the Benedick and Beatrice plot, if it can be said in a word, turns on misprision. They are "both gulled by hearsay". Bertrand Evans, in his consideration of the play in *Shakespeare's Comedies*, agrees but writes: "Each was won to love the other through a humane and noble sympathy which was not dimmed but made more luminous by error." Barbara Everett's essay '*Much Ado About Nothing*', *Critical Quarterly*, 1961, is about the dominance of woman's world in the play. J. R. Mulryne, in his recent study *Much Ado About Nothing*, emphasizes the need for "a theatre-conscious reading of the text".

Othello

It is impossible to study the great tragedies of Shakespeare without an encounter with the views of A. C. Bradley, so one might just as well begin with his *Shakespearean Tragedy* in which *Othello* is the subject of the sixth lecture. William Empson, in his *The Structure of Complex Words*, has a famous section, among others equally well-known, on the use of the word "honest" in *Othello*, which Empson considers the key word of the play. He writes "The fifty two uses of *honest* and *honesty* in *Othello* are a very queer business; there is no other play in which Shakespeare worries a word like that." Iago has fascinated the public even more than Othello. Maud Bodkin (in her *Archetypal Patterns in Poetry*) writes in the essay 'The Hero and the Devil': "I shall attempt some study of the tragedy of *Othello*, in order to examine the figure of Iago in relation to Othello, in order to compare it with Mephistopheles in relation to Faust." Leonard F. Dean has published a collection of essays on *Othello*, entitled *Casebook on Othello*. Helen Gardner, in a short essay entitled 'The Noble Moor'

which has been reprinted in Ann Ridler's *Shakespearean Criticism,
1935–1960*, justifies Shakespeare against the Rhymer school of
critics whose views impressed T. S. Eliot. F. R. Leavis, in his
'Diabolic intellect and the Noble Hero', included in his *The Common
Pursuit*, blames Othello for his own undoing; though I think
that Sir Lawrence Olivier's interpretation of the part was nearer
the mark, showing Othello to be a man made mad by suspicion
and having no companion with wit enough to be able to release
him from the tyranny of his obsession. Desdemona's love in the
end released him, but at the cost of both their lives. When great
men lose their wits, it is rare that only two or three must die.

Pericles

I like D. A. Traversi's study of this play which is contained in
his book *Shakespeare: the last phase* and also in part in Boris
Ford's collection of essays *The Age of Shakespeare*. Traversi says
that the plot of *Pericles* hinges on those lines spoken by Pericles
to greet the birth of his child, which has cost the life of Thaisa, his
wife, on a storm-bound ship:

> Now, mild may be thy life!
> For a more blustrous birth had never babe:
> Quiet and gentle thy conditions! for
> Thou art the rudeliest welcome to this world
> That ever was prince's child. Happy what follows!
> Thou hast as chiding a nativity
> As fire, air, water, earth and heaven can make,
> To herald thee from the womb.

In these lines Traversi sees "the characteristic Shakespearean
intuition of subsistent continuity, the sense that birth and death,
tempest and following calm, are in reality related aspects of a
single process to which the elements themselves—'fire, air, water,'
and even 'earth and heaven'—are, in their universal presence,
witnesses."

Richard II

Eugene M. Waith's collection *Shakespeare: the histories* is a most convenient source of information on these plays. A recent study of *Richard II* by A. R. Humphreys says: "The beauty of Richard's poetry . . . cannot be denied . . . but the play is equally about the importance of good rule and the moral dilemmas presented by injustice." E. M. W. Tillyard's *Shakespeare's History Plays* emphasizes the medievalism of *Richard II*, whose world was one in which means, exactly followed, were more important than ends. There are many fascinating essays of which I. Ribner's 'Bolingbroke, a true Machievellian', *Modern Language Quarterly*, IX, 1948, demonstrates the arrival of the new ruthless Renaissance magnate into the world of the medieval kings.

Richard III

Peter Alexander's *Shakespeare's Henry VI and Richard III* is mainly concerned to establish the text and to point to Shakespeare's originality in these early plays. There have not been studies of the quality of Sir Lawrence Olivier's interpretation of the role in his film. W. H. Clemen has an essay 'Tradition and originality in Shakespeare's *Richard III*' in *Shakespeare Quarterly*, V, 1954.

Romeo and Juliet

"Nothing in this highly-sexed world seems to damage the intense purity of Juliet's anticipation of the 'amorous rites' that are to be 'Played for a pair of stainless maidenhoods'. Again and again the innocence of the lovers is emphasised." So writes T. J. B. Spencer in his introduction to his *New Penguin Shakespeare* edition of the play. Spencer's criticism has all the directness of Juliet and all the eloquence of Romeo. A very interesting study of the power of Shakespeare's punning to "clarify the conflict of incompatible truths" is contained in M. M. Mahood's *Shakespeare's Wordplay*. He quotes Romeo, after he has drunk the poison,

O true apothecary!
Thy drugs are quick. Thus with a kiss I die.

The words "true" and "quick" with their complex of meanings exactly maintain that "tragic equilibrium" of understanding that Romeo has achieved.

Professor Spencer, in his section on 'Further reading', recommends the essay '*Romeo and Juliet* as an experimental tragedy' (in H. B. Charlton's *Shakespearean Tragedy*) and 'In defence of Mercutio' (in Leslie Hotson's *Shakespeare's Sonnets Dated and Other Essays*) as well as several others perhaps not so readily available. Harley Granville-Barker's *Preface* to the play is, of course, essential to an understanding of the problems of the staging of the play.

Taming of the Shrew

G. I. Duthie's *Shakespeare* contains a long essay in interpretation of this play. H. B. Charlton's essay in his *Shakespearean Comedy* considers the play anti-romantic, and E. M. W. Tillyard's essay in his *Shakespeare: the early comedies* sees Petruchio in a double role, as a brute, and as a bringer of Katherine to self-knowledge. The key to the play would seem, in Zeffirelli's film, to be "Kiss me, Kate", and Petruchio to be consistently in love with her, his brutality no more than a means to an end, and no more than is made necessary by Kate's own stormy personality. Cecil C. Seronsy suggests '*Supposes* as the unifying theme in *The Taming of the Shrew*', *Shakespeare Quarterly*, XIV, 1963. Bertrand Evans in his *Shakespeare's Comedies* has some commentary on the richly comic sub-plot.

The Tempest

Frank Kermode's introduction to his *Arden* edition of the play is frequently referred to as one of the best available commentaries. An essay by Dean Ebner in *Shakespeare Quarterly*, XVI, 1965, entitled '*The Tempest*: rebellion and the ideal state', asks the question, Why does Shakespeare introduce such a large body of Montaigne's ideas nearly word for word into *The Tempest*?, and answers that he is concerned to refute Montaigne's view of the noble savage as expounded by Gonzalo through the words of Prospero. G. Wilson Knight writes of *The Tempest* in his *The Crown of Life* as "an expression of the Renaissance imagination under pressure from British puritanism". Knight says that the "most careful and important study" of the play "hitherto" is Colin Still's *The Timeless Theme*, which was originally published under the title *Shakespeare's Mystery Play*. Sir E. K. Chambers's chapter 'The integrity of *The Tempest*', in *Shakespearean Gleanings*, like all his short essays, is most enlightening. W. H. Auden's verse commentary on the play, *The Sea and the Mirror*, published in 1945 in his book *For the Time Being*, is caviar for the general.

Timon of Athens

A short essay by A. S. Collins appeared in the *Review of English Studies*, XXII, 1946, entitled '*Timon of Athens*: a reconsideration', and led the way to the establishing of this play's reputation for our generation. Previously it had been taken for a piece of sound and fury signifying, what? Una Ellis-Fermor has written of the play in *Shakespeare the Dramatist*, edited by K. Muir, her essay being entitled '*Timon of Athens*: an unfinished play'. This essay appeared in *Review of English Studies*, XVIII, 1942. *The New Cambridge* edition of 1957 has an introduction by the editor, J. C. Maxwell, making an extended comparison of Lear and Timon. There have been several notable essays in recent years of which there is space to mention only one, that by E. A. J. Honigmann, '*Timon of Athens*', *Shakespeare Quarterly*, XII, 1961.

Titus Andronicus

E. M. W. Tillyard, in his *Shakespeare's History Plays*, has a short section on this play in which he refutes T. S. Eliot's judgement that *Titus* "is one of the stupidest and most uninspired plays ever written", and points to the "strong political trends" of the play and praises the quality of the verse. The play is also considered in M. C. Bradbrook's *Shakespeare and Elizabethan Poetry*, and in A. Sommers's ' "Wilderness of Tigers": structure and symbolism in *Titus Andronicus*', *Essays in Criticism*, X, 1960.

Troilus and Cressida

John Keats had a great admiration for this play, and Dr. Johnson considered it very correctly written, but modern critics have been pleased to class it as a 'problem' play. M. C. Bradbrook explains 'What Shakespeare did to Chaucer's *Troilus and Cressida*', *Shakespeare Quarterly*, IX, 1958. O. J. Campbell's *Comicall Satyre and Shakespeare's 'Troilus and Cressida'* contains an analysis of the play that has never been seriously challenged. The play is discussed in Theodore Spencer's *Shakespeare and the Nature of Man*. G. Wilson Knight's essay 'The Philosophy of *Troilus and Cressida*' is included in his *The Wheel of Fire*. W. Empson has some interesting things to say about the play in his *Some Versions of Pastoral*. A recent essay by Robert Kimbrough— 'Shakespeare's *Troilus and Cressida* and its setting'—analyses the themes of the play.

Twelfth Night

Perhaps the way to start a study of this play is by reading L. Hotson's *The First Night of 'Twelfth Night'*, which is a most detailed account of the probable first performance of the play. Of recent essays, the one I like best and which seems to me to be in the trend of the most significant and sensible Shakespeare criticism of today, is Barbara K. Lewalski's 'Thematic pattern in *Twelfth Night*', *Shakespeare Studies*, I, 1965, in which she develops, with reference to Shakespeare's use of his Biblical knowledge, "central themes and motifs of this play" pointing out that they "contain something of the religious significance associated with Epiphany and with the spirit of Christmastide". L. G. Salingar has an essay on 'The design of *Twelfth Night*' in *Shakespeare Quarterly*, IX, 1958. The play is brilliantly treated in C. L. Barber's *Shakespeare's Festive Comedy*.

Two Gentlemen of Verona

Mario Praz has an interesting essay on 'Shakespeare's Italy' in *Shakespeare Survey*, VII, 1954. J. F. Danby writes of 'Shakespeare criticism and *Two Gentlemen of Verona*' in *Critical Quarterly*, II, 1960. O. J. Campbell's early essay '*The Two Gentlemen of Verona* and Italian Comedy' in *Michigan Studies in Shakespeare, Milton and Donne*, 1925. Stanley Wells, in *Shakespeare Jahrbuch*, XCIX, 1963, writes of 'The failure of *Two Gentlemen of Verona*', and Harold Brooks, in *Essays and Studies*, XVI, 1963, has a quaintly titled essay 'Two clowns in a comedy (to say nothing of a dog): Speed, Launce (and Crab) in *Two Gentlemen of Verona*.'

The Winter's Tale

E. M. W. Tillyard suggested in his *Shakespeare's Last Plays* that Shakespeare attempted in *The Winter's Tale* to compress the whole scheme of Dante's *Divine Comedy* into a single play—Acts I–III are Leontes 'Hell', self-created and self-sustained; then from the end of Act III to the beginning of Act V is the Purgatory, 16 years of penance and repentance, and then, finally, comes the Paradiso of family reunion. In his essay 'The structural pattern of *The Winter's Tale*,' *Review of English Literature*, V, 1964, Ernest Schanzer examines the role of Perdita in Act IV, and attempts a different interpretation, comparing the play with the similarly structured *Pericles*. Another interesting recent essay is Inga-Stina Ewbank's 'Triumph of Time in *The Winter's Tale*', *Review of English Literature*, V, 1964, in which she examines the play as a "dramatic exploration of the manifold meanings of Time". The play juxtaposes past and present across a gap of 16 years, and although the dramatic technique aims at an effect of timelessness (by the use of deliberate anachronisms, for instance), Time is the controlling and shaping figure behind the dramatic structure, and, "paradoxically, Time has at last in its triumph brought about its own defeat". John Lawlor, in his essay 'Pandosto and the nature of dramatic romance', *Studies in English Drama*, presented to Baldwin Maxwell, *Philological Quarterly*, XLI, 1962, remarks "the way forward is the step into redoubled fiction", and shows how this technique was carried to an unequalled point of achievement in *The Winter's Tale*. A. D. Nuttall's *Shakespeare: 'The Winter's Tale'* is a fresh and stimulating analysis in which he writes "to allegorise a play into a metaphysical system is to smooth off its corners". S. L. Bethell wrote *The Winter's Tale: A Study* and J. D. Wilson gave his views in his introduction to the New Cambridge edition of the play.

Finally, a word about the invaluable *A Select Shakespeare Bibliography* by J. R. Brown published in 1962 in which careful selections from the available studies in books and journals is given play by play.

The Shakespeare Apocrypha

The accepted Shakespeare canon is the thirty-seven plays printed in the First Folio by Heminge and Condell in 1623. The Third Folio in 1663 also included six other plays which had appeared in quarto editions bearing Shakespeare's name or initials; these were *Locrine*, *Sir John Oldcastle*, *Thomas Lord Cromwell*, *The London Prodigal*, *The Puritan*, and *A Yorkshire Tragedy*. A book which outlines the argument of four of these and gives an account of critical opinion on them through the centuries is *Studies in the Shakespeare Apocrypha* by Baldwin Maxwell, who concludes himself that none of them are by Shakespeare. Three source plays, those for *King John*, *The Taming of the Shrew*, and *Henry V* are held by some critics to be early work of Shakespeare. But there are three plays in which most authorities are agreed that Shakespeare at least had a hand; these are *Two Noble Kinsmen*, *Sir Thomas More*, and *Edward III*. The first and third of these, together with the play *Pericles*, which is included in the First Folio but is thought to have been only partly Shakespeare's work by some critics, are discussed in Kenneth Muir's book *Shakespeare as Collaborator*, in which the method of image-clusters to identify Shakespearean passages is used.

One of the source plays already mentioned, *The Famous Victories of Henry V*, is studied by Seymour M. Pitcher in his *The Case for Shakespeare's Authorship of The Famous Victories*, which prints a complete text of the anonymous play. The text of all these plays, attributed in part or in whole to Shakespeare, and that of several others, is usefully presented in C. F. Tucker Brooke's *The Shakespeare Apocrypha*, described by the author as "being a collection of fourteen plays which have been ascribed to Shakespeare, together with critical and supplementary matter".

CHAPTER 10

The Bibliographical Apparatus

THERE are two libraries, one in England and one in the United States, devoted to the collection of every imaginable item relevant to the study of Shakespeare. Needless to say, by far the more impressive of the two is the Folger Shakespeare Library on Capitol Hill in Washington, D.C. Opened in 1932, this library contains the comprehensive collection made by Henry Clay Folger, one-time chairman of the Board of the Standard Oil Company of New York, with the help of his wife, Emily Clara Jordan. It is richly endowed, the funds being administered by trustees of Amherst College. A short account of the library and its resources, which exist "for the promotion and diffusion of knowledge in regard to the history and writings of Shakespeare" may be found in the first volume of *Shakespeare Survey*. The Trustees of Amherst College published in 1933 a book by Joseph Quincy Adams entitled *The Folger Shakespeare Library*. Since then the library has attracted countless scholars, and by endowing fellowships has encouraged much research.

The Shakespeare Memorial Library in Birmingham, England, is administered by the Birmingham City Library. An 8-page pamphlet describing this collection is available on request from the City Librarian. This library attempts to obtain some record of every English and foreign Shakespeare production, including gramophone records and radio and television scripts. Each year the librarian provides for *Shakespeare Survey* a list of the year's Shakespeare productions. The library possesses editions of the plays in sixty languages and a virtually complete collection of modern books with even a remote bearing on the study of

Shakespeare and his age. In addition there are thousands of en-gravings and illustrations in the collection—contained in over 200 indexed scrapbooks. There are also 52 volumes of playbills.

The Shakespeare Institute, founded by Professor Allardyce Nicoll in 1951, is a centre for postgraduate studies and is part of the Department of English Language and Literature of the University of Birmingham. It is housed in two buildings, one at Stratford-upon-Avon and one on the university campus at Edgbaston, Birmingham. At Stratford at the Shakespeare Centre are the collections of the Shakespeare Birthplace Trust and of the Royal Shakespeare Theatre. These collections include a collection of editions of Shakespeare from the First Folio onwards and well-indexed archives, rich in historical and biographical works. The Institute is justly proud of its detailed Chronological Index of books printed before 1640, its Register of theatrical performances, unpublished concordances of some Elizabethan and Jacobean writers, and collections of photographs of early paintings, engrav-ings, costumes, and furnishings.

There are great manuscript riches available at the Bodleian Library in Oxford, but perhaps the finest collection of dramatic material bearing upon Shakespeare is to be found in the city of Edinburgh. An exhibition of printed books to mark the quarter-centenary of Shakespeare's birth was held in the National Library of Scotland and in the University Library in Edinburgh in 1964. These books were all drawn from the resources of these two libra-ries, and the catalogue of the exhibition lists 141 items. As J. Dover Wilson explains in his introduction to this catalogue that the University Library possesses in the Halliwell–Phillips Collec-tion and other stock most of the great editions of Shakespeare, including some of those appearing in the early nineteenth century which are not usually accessible elsewhere. In the National Library is the Bute Collection, the nucleus of which was collected by Lady Mary Wortley Montagu and given by her to her daughter, the Countess of Bute.

A list of the Shakespeare holdings of the two Edinburgh libraries is to be found in vol. 15 of *Studies in Bibliography*, the papers of the Bibliographical Society of the University of Virginia. It was prepared by Miss Marion Linton of the staff of the National Library of Scotland. As she explains, this list is intended as an appendix to Greg's *Bibliography of the English Printed Drama to the Restoration* which is the starting point for all bibliographical research into the drama of this period. Greg's work was followed up by the publication in 1939 of Bartlett and Pollard's *Census of Shakespeare's Plays in Quarto, 1594–1709.*

The Huntingdon Library in San Marino, California, although not devoted entirely to Shakespeare, has a very considerable collection of works valuable to the study of his writings, including original copies of nearly all the books that it is now generally agreed were probably read by Shakespeare himself. An account of the holdings of this library is to be found in *Shakespeare Survey 6* by Godfrey Davies.

The first considerable bibliography of Shakespeare was published in 1911. The author, W. Jaggard, entitled his work *Shakespeare Bibliography: a dictionary of every known issue of the writings of our national poet and of recorded opinion thereon in the English language.* A far more massive collection, however, is *A Shakespeare Bibliography* by Walther Ebisch and Levin L. Schücking, published in 1931, with a supplement covering the years 1930–5 and a further supplement, on similar principles by Gordon Ross Smith, entitled *A Classified Shakespeare Bibliography,* covering the years 1936–58. Ebisch and Schücking divided the field into the following sections: Bibliography, Elizabethan literature; Shakespeare's life; Shakespeare's personality; Text: transmission and emendation; Shakespeare's sources, literary influence, and cultural relations; the art of Shakespeare, language, vocabulary, prosody, and style; Shakespeare's dramatic art; Shakespeare's stage and production of his plays; Literary taste in Shakespeare's time; Aesthetic criticism of Shakespeare; Shakespeare's influence through the centuries; Civilization in Shakespeare's England; Shakespeare controversies; the Works, chronology, individual dramas, poems, apocrypha. This analysis is itself quite a contribution to scholarship, and as each section is carefully subdivided the contents page of the bibliography serves as an orderly review of the whole field of Shakespeare studies. Listed in these 3 volumes are not only books, but also articles and papers that have appeared in a vast number of journals and periodicals. Yet despite the quantity of material listed, Ebisch and Schücking make it plain in their introduction that their list is *selective*, since not everything they have met with in their researches do they consider of value for what they term "the scientific study of Shakespeare".

For publications after 1958, recourse must be had to the *Library of Congress Catalogue: a cumulative list of works represented on Library of Congress printed cards. Books. Subjects.* Since 1960 this massive catalogue has been published yearly; previously cumulations appeared every 5 years. Entries under 'Shakespeare' are arranged in an alphabetical subject sequence; there are something like fifty subject headings, as well as separate headings for each of the plays and poems, so a search can be narrowed down to a definite subject heading and is assisted by cross-references from headings not used. Items cited include films and filmstrips and chapters on Shakespeare from the published proceedings of learned societies. Full bibliographical details are given for each work. New editions of the plays in all languages, with details printed in the language of the publication, are listed in the *National Union Catalogue*, a cumulated author list made up from the Library of Congress printed cards and titles reported from other American libraries, which is compiled and published quarterly by the Library of Congress. The *British Museum Subject Index of Books Acquired* lists books about Shakespeare under the subject heading 'English literature'. The latest volumes cover the years 1956–60. The British National Bibliography's *Cumulated Subject Catalogue* appears every 5 years. The most recent to appear, with the printing arranged in three column pages for the first time, covers the years 1960–4. This catalogue lists in Dewey Decimal classified order all the books deposited in the British Museum Library under the provisions of the Copyright Act, and is therefore limited to British publications and those foreign books handled in Britain by British publishers. Works about Shakespeare

are arranged according to a scheme devised by the B.N.B. editors. This scheme lists books under a number of subject headings and sub-headings, a more complex system than that operated by the Library of Congress.

Papers and articles and reviews printed in the periodicals and journals are recorded each year in *Shakespeare Survey* in a narrative survey of the year's work, details of author, title, and journal being given in the footnotes. *The Annual Bibliography of English Language and Literature* published by the Modern Humanities Research Association of Downing College, Cambridge, has a section in each annual volume devoted to Shakespeare, listing all the items published during the year, including books, papers, and articles and review articles and unpublished doctoral dissertations. Each item has a reference number and the entry gives author, title, journal, volume, and page references. This bibliography is faithfully published year by year but has slipped 2 years, so that the volume for 1965 appeared in the autumn of 1967. The most up-to-date record of journal articles is to be found in the *Essay and General Literature Index* published by the H. W. Wilson Company of New York. This indexes not only periodicals but also the items in published collections of essays and miscellaneous works. Another American index is the *Social Science and Humanities Index*, formerly the *International Index*, which is published annually and lists items on Shakespeare by subject such as 'Humor', 'Imagery', and so on. This index cites items from a number of British journals, such as *New Statesman* and *Encounter*. In Britain, the Library Association publishes *The British Humanities Index* in which Shakespeare items are listed. This index dates from 1962 when the old *Subject Index to Periodicals*, which began publication in 1915 and was continued until 1961 with a gap from 1923–5, was divided into three parts. The original *Poole's Index to Periodical Literature* began publication in 1882, and supplements were produced regularly to carry the venture on until 1907. So much of the work on Shakespeare is done in the United States that an exclusively British index is of only marginal value to the Shakespeare student today.

In 1965 the University of Cincinnati began publication of

Shakespeare Studies which is planned to be an annual collection of "research, criticism and reviews". It is edited by J. Leeds Barroll. It has a valuable section of 'Abstracts of articles and monographs of current interest' which gives more details of papers than the annual review in *Shakespeare Survey*. The English Association's *Year's Work in English Studies* sets aside a chapter, up to 50 pages long, to consider Shakespeare studies under the following heads: Editions, Commemorative publications; General works and collections of essays, including foreign publications; Editions of individual plays and poems; Theatre and acting; Criticism and scholarship. Taken year by year, along with the review in *Shakespeare Survey*, the student can trace the development of Shakespeare studies with considerable accuracy and is unlikely to miss any work of significance.

So much for keeping up to date with what is being produced; now for a look at the problem of reviewing what has been done in the past. Ebisch and Schücking have done this on a vast scale, but the student would be grateful for a review contained within a more modest compass. The 60 pages of double column print which carry the Shakespeare items in the first volume of the *Cambridge Bibliography of English Literature*, edited by F. W. Bateson, list both books and articles and divides the list into the familiar sections. Merely to read the titles in this bibliography is itself a minor education. A supplement was published in 1957, edited by George Watson, which contained a further 34 pages of Shakespeare items. George Watson has also edited the *Concise Cambridge Bibliography of English Literature, 600–1950*, in which the number of pages on Shakespeare is reduced to four. The *London Library Catalogues* are very useful for the lists of Shakespeare material they contain. The first was published in 1914, with supplements for 1910–11, 1913–20, 1920–8 and 1928–50. First, the editions of the plays in the library's stock are listed and then, under the heading 'References', appear works of criticism, commentary and interpretation, biography, and history. These are arranged in alphabetical order of author, which makes the catalogue less easy to use than the subject lists of the Library of Congress subject catalogue already mentioned. Volume 220 of the *British Museum*

Catalogue carries over 550 columns of entries on Shakespeare, including works in many languages, details printed in the language of the publication, arranged according to the B.M. scheme for Shakespeare. This is probably the most useful list for the older works of scholarship. For works in print, reference should be made to Bowker's *Subject Guide to Books in Print* for work available in the U.S.A., and to Whitaker's *British Books in Print* for those in print in Britain. The former catalogue lists items by subject, but the latter has only author and title lists, although the titles are so arranged that the maximum use may be made of the words of the title to act as a subject index.

A number of general reference books contain very useful bibliographies. *Companion to Shakespeare Studies*, edited by Harley Granville-Barker and G. B. Harrison, has a 21-page list of books with careful short annotations. This list was compiled in the 1930's but most of the items are still often quoted. *Shakespeare: the writer and his work*, edited by Bonamy Dobrée, is a collection of essays sponsored by the British Council, and contains a *Select Shakespeare Bibliography* by J. R. Brown, which brings the story up to the 1950's. The most recently published lists are contained in *A Shakespeare Encyclopaedia*, edited by Oscar James Campbell and Edward G. Quinn. This is by far the most comprehensive single-volume work of reference available; each of the plays is separately treated under such headings as 'Text', 'Sources', 'Comment', 'Stage History', and a list of references is included. In addition one of the appendixes is a compact bibliography covering the whole field of studies of Shakespeare. F. E. Halliday, in his more modest *A Shakespeare Companion, 1564–1964*, available as a paper-back, gives a 20-page bibliography, arranged in eight sections. Unfortunately, there are very few annotations and the lists are too long to be of much use to the student who cannot distinguish between the importance of an Empson and a Stopes, but make a good check list for someone wanting to review the productions of any particular group of Shakespeare scholars.

Ronald Berman of the University of California, San Diego, has published a readable survey entitled *Reader's Guide to Shakespeare's*

Plays: a discursive bibliography. This book is a selective bibliography of criticism and scholarship for all the plays. It gives brief descriptions of the books, and also of the articles published in journals, which the author considers worthy of notice. He himself has made his own contributions in this field.

Three periodical publications which give notices of new recordings on long-playing records, new films and television performances, and new books, are, firstly, *Shakespeare Newsletter* which appears five times a year under the editorship of Louis Marder; second; *Shakespeare Quarterly*, edited by J. G. McManaway, which is a learned academic review, about two-thirds of its contents being devoted to recent papers of Shakespeare scholarship, and one-third to reviews of new books; and, thirdly, the *Shakespeare Jahrbuch*, published in Heidelberg.

In the Summer Number of *Shakespeare Quarterly*, 1965, is printed 'Shakespeare: an annotated bibliography for 1964'— Robert W. Dent, editor; Rudolph E. Habernicht, associate editor, aided by a committee of twenty-seven correspondents throughout the world. This bibliography lists 3270 items in many languages and includes minutiae like a 12-page booklist published by the St. Pancras Borough Library. The editors write in their introduction: "The following bibliography, which includes only works directly relating to Shakespeare, attempts to list all items of interest to the scholar, the actor and producer, and the general reader." They claim to have included a representative selection of items published in journals. There is a comprehensive and valuable index which collects under the heading 'Shakespeare' a wide range of analytical entries. The bibliography is prepared under fifteen headings, which themselves are a useful guide to Shakespeare studies, defining areas of research, namely; annuals and special issues; bibliographies and surveys; editions; selections and adaptations; celebrations and tributes; libraries and collections; Shakespeare around the world; Shakespeare's life and times; sources; textual bibliography; interpretation and evaluation; Shakespeare and the arts; Shakespeare in elementary and secondary schools; Shakespeare in the theatre; films, radio, television, recordings.

Gramophone Recordings of Shakespeare's Works

THE Argo Record Company have issued recordings of the Complete Works of William Shakespeare uncut in the text of the *New Shakespeare*, edited for the Syndics of the Cambridge University Press by John Dover Wilson and recorded by the Marlow Dramatic Society and professional players directed by George Rylands, the whole enterprise being under the auspices of the British Council. In addition, there are available from the Argo Company four recordings of Scenes from Shakespeare, two from the tragedies, and one each from the comedies and histories. Some of the recordings are available for stereo as well as mono.

Caedmon Records and the Shakespeare Recording Society have produced a number of items. The following plays are available on mono: *The Tempest*; *The Two Gentlemen of Verona*; *The Merry Wives of Windsor*; *Measure for Measure*; *Much Ado About Nothing*; *A Midsummer-Night's Dream*; *The Merchant of Venice*; *As You Like It*; *The Taming of the Shrew*; *All's Well That Ends Well*; *Twelfth Night*; *The Winter's Tale*; *King John*; *King Richard II*; *King Henry IV, Parts I and II*; *Othello*; *Coriolanus*; *Titus Andronicus*; *Romeo and Juliet*; *Julius Caesar*; *Macbeth*; *Hamlet*; *King Lear*; *Troylus and Cressida*; *Antony and Cleopatra*; *Cymbeline* and *The Sonnets* (read by Sir John Gielgud); *Venus and Adonis* and *A Lover's Complaint*, and *The Rape of Lucrece* (read by Richard Burton), and other poems (read by Dame Edith Evans and Sir Donald Wolfit). In addition there is *Shakespeare—Soul of an Age*, a collection of excerpts from some of the plays, and *The Poetry of Shakespeare*, readings of a few of the sonnets and some of the poems from the plays. There is a recording of Dylan Thomas reading from *King Lear* and of Sir John Gielgud reading a collection of extracts from the plays and sonnets.

Spoken Arts, founded in 1956, is producing a collection of high quality recordings from literature. These are marketed by Mc-Graw-Hill. Shakespeare is represented by 50-minute abridgements of *Hamlet*; *Macbeth*; *Othello*; *King Lear*; *Julius Caesar*; *The Merchant of Venice*—presented by players of the Dublin Gate Theatre; and *Romeo and Juliet*; *Henry IV, Parts I and II*; and *Henry V*—presented by the Swan Theatre Players. *As You Like It*; *Midsummer Night's Dream*; *Much Ado About Nothing*; *The Taming of the Shrew*; *The Tempest*; *Twelfth Night*; *The Comedy of Errors*; *Cymbeline*; *Richard II*; *Richard III*; *Troilus and Cressida*; *The Two Gentlemen of Verona*; and *The Winter's Tale* are similarly available, recorded by the Folio Theatre Players. In addition, Paul Rogers of the Old Vic has recorded *Scenes from Shakespeare*, and Anew McMaster and his Shakespearean Company have recorded scenes from nine of the plays, namely *Taming of the Shrew, Othello, Merchant of Venice, Romeo and Juliet, Julius Caesar, King Lear, Hamlet,* and *As You Like It*. There are also recordings of *Venus and Adonis*; *The Rape of Lucrece*; *Songs from Shakespeare's Plays*, and *Love in Shakespeare*; an anthology presented by E. Martin Browne and Henzie Raeburn; and a series of *Soliloquies and Scenes for Actors*, presented by Michael Mac-Liammoir and Hilton Edwards of the Dublin Gate Theatre.

Gramophone Magazine notes new recordings and each year publishes an index of the year's recordings. There is also available a classical recordings index.

APPENDIX II

List of periodicals in which articles and notices of interest to students of Shakespeare may be found (including some which have ceased publication)

Abstract of English Studies
American Historical Review
American Journal of Philology
Baconiana
Bulletin of Hispanic Studies
Bulletin of the John Rylands Library
Cambridge Abstracts
Cambridge Journal
Cambridge Review
Cambridge Quarterly
Centennial Review
Classical Review
College English
Cornhill Magazine
Contemporary Review
Critical Quarterly
Dissertation Abstracts
Educational Theatre Journal
ELH (Journal of English Literary History)
Encounter
English
English Historical Review
English Language Notes
English Review
English Studies
Essays and Studies

Essays in Criticism
Études Anglaises
Explicator
Fortnightly Review
Guardian (formerly *The Manchester Guardian*)
Huntingdon Library Quarterly
Jacobean Theatre
Journal of English and Germanic Philology
Journal of the History of Ideas
Journal of Modern History
Kenyon Review
The Library: Transactions of the Bibliographical Society
Life and Letters
Listener
Literature and Psychology
Modern Language Journal
Modern Language Notes
Modern Language Quarterly
Modern Language Review
Modern Philology
Neophilologus
New Republic
New Statesman
New York Herald Tribune Book Review
Notes and Queries
Observer
Oxford Abstracts
Papers in English Language and Literature
Papers of the Bibliographical Society of America
Philological Quarterly
Publications of the Modern Language Association of America
Quarterly Review
Renaissance News
Review of English Literature
Review of English Studies
Saturday Review of Literature

Scrutiny
Sewanee Review
Shakespeare Association Bulletin
Shakespeare Newsletter
Shakespeare Quarterly
Studies in Bibliography
Studies in English Literature
Studies in Philology
Sunday Times
Texas Studies in Language and Literature
Theatre Arts
Theatre Notebook
Times Literary Supplement
Times Saturday Review
Transactions of the Royal Society of Literature
University of Toronto Quarterly
University of Texas Studies in English
Yale Review

Index of Works Cited